Illustrated Dictionary
of Automobile
Body Styles

Illustrated Dictionary of Automobile Body Styles

Lennart W. Haajanen

Illustrations by Bertil Nydén

Foreword by Karl Ludvigsen

McFarland & Company, Inc., Publishers
Jefferson, North Carolina, and London

The present work is a reprint of the illustrated case bound edition of Illustrated Dictionary of Automobile Body Styles, *first published in 2003 by McFarland.*

LIBRARY OF CONGRESS CATALOGUING-IN-PUBLICATION DATA

Haajanen, Lennart W., 1932–
Illustrated dictionary of automobile body styles
/ Lennart W. Haajanen ; illustrations by Bertil Nydén ;
foreword by Karl Ludvigsen.
p.   cm.
Includes bibliographical references.

ISBN-13: 978-0-7864-3737-5
softcover : 50 # alkaline paper ∞

1. Automobiles—Bodies—History—Dictionaries.
2. Industrial design—Dictionaries. I. Title.
TL9 .H23   2008   629.2'6'09—dc21   2002014546

British Library cataloguing data are available

Cover photograph ©2002 Corbis Images

Manufactured in the United States of America

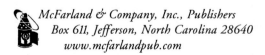

*McFarland & Company, Inc., Publishers
Box 611, Jefferson, North Carolina 28640
www.mcfarlandpub.com*

To the memory of Denis Jenkinson, motorsports journalist of the old style *Motor Sport* (London) magazine.

Acknowledgments

When thinking back on all the individuals who have shown interest, given their time and contributed in various ways to my work I should like first of all to put on record my gratitude to the late Andy Rheault of the American Bugatti Club, who so kindly and unselfishly provided me with important information and comment relating to many body styles and subsequently put me into contact with Christopher Foster just before passing away. Kit Foster, again most efficient and helpful, apart from studying my manuscript and offering valuable comments and advice, also readily answered some queries that arose in the course of research and writing.

I am indebted to my great friend Björn Linn for studying the whole manuscript and for most generously lending to me many books from his vast library. Likewise, my thanks are due to my friend Michael Wheildon, who studied the manuscript from a British point of view at an early stage. Both Björn and Michael offered many valuable suggestions, and I have in fact included verbatim one or two of those offered by Michael.

My sincerest thanks are due to my friends Claes Rydholm and Anders Hörlén, who have been instrumental and indefatigable in keeping my project in mind throughout the whole period, from starting to write the manuscript to this day

and from time to time providing me with articles, magazines, and snippets and suggesting suitable reference literature.

I have also a great sense of obligation to the following individuals and friends in various parts of the world for helping me explain specific term origins and their correct spellings, alternatively referring me to sources for further study: Gyula Burányi (Hungarian), Bengt Dieden (French), Francesco Guasti (Italian), Hans A. Koch (German, French and Italian), Alexandr Pankow (Russian), François Pianetti (Italian), Neil Purdy (German), Ernie Robibero (American English), Albert Schulhof (Czech) and Lorentz Österling (French).

Finally, my special appreciation is due to Sylvia Roberts for advice on my English in certain parts of the book, to Staffan Lindhé and Gunnar Stenmar for their good advice and continued encouragement relating to manuscript administration and publishers, to Tommy Blomquist for lending me rare carriage literature, to Christer Mellin for providing articles (among them important ones relating to "GTO"), to Marián Šuman-Hreblay for furnishing glossaries and, not least, to Vinko Katic for keeping my computer going.

Fall 2002

Contents

Foreword

by Karl Ludvigsen

The world's car makers are rediscovering their heritages. Once-dormant marques such as Bugatti, Maybach and even Isotta-Fraschini are being revived. Those who are fortunate enough to have a heritage—including BMW, Mercedes-Benz, Alfa Romeo and Fiat, among others—are celebrating them both publicly and privately.

The public celebrations help communicate the character and values of their marques to a public to whom heritage indicates solidity, stability and reliability. Those companies that enjoy a heritage like to deploy them to distinguish their enterprises, their products, from those of the Japanese, Koreans and Malaysians—relative newcomers to the world's roster of auto makers.

The private celebrations take place internally to stimulate designers and marketers of cars to think creatively about ways to exploit a company's heritage in the characteristics of their products and the ways in which they are sold. Past products and traditions can provide powerful inspiration for future ventures. There's only one problem. Many designers and engineers are far too young to have any meaningful memory of those earlier autos and events. They need to gain second-hand inspiration from museums, rallies, exhibitions and books—like this one.

Even in the Y2K era of proliferating body styles and niche models the stunning diversity of body elements and details recorded and revealed in Lennart Haajanen's book will come as a revelation to today's generation of car planners and designers. No matter how knowledgeable they consider themselves to be, among the broughams, town cars, torpedoes, landaulets, skiffs and salamancas depicted and described in these pages they will find surprising and ingenious interpretations of the automobile's shape and structure.

It is entertaining to think of the new kinds of cars for the future that might be inspired by Haajanen's thorough research and clear presentation. What about a "buggy," for example? We could do with a light, high-wheeled and efficient road vehicle. Or the "rumble" or "dickey" seat. I well remember clambering into the seat in the rear deck of my mother's 1935 Ford convertible. Would a rumble seat for the 2000s be possible? Or would it fall afoul of the ever-watchful safety vigilantes?

It's enjoyable too to see how the names of prominent people are associated with body designs. Pietro Bordino was one of the great stars of Fiat's Grand Prix team, racing some of the first cars with pointed streamlined tails designed with the help of Fiat's aeronautical department. How appropriate that a pointed-tail body became known as a "Bordino." Another style was named after its originator, Lord Brougham. For many years

Ford's London offices were in the elegant terraced house once owned by Brougham.

One of the most evocative names is "speedster," celebrated particularly by the gorgeous Auburns. Now it seems that Porsche considers "speedster" its property, objecting as it did to the use of that name by Opel for a sports car. Perhaps that's only a fair exchange. Porsche has seen one of its body-style names move into the public domain. After its successes in the Sicilian Targa Florio road race it used the "Targa" name for a new 1967 model with a removable roof section over the passengers. Now any such roof is known generically as a "Targa" top.

Most intriguing for me has been the opportunity offered by this book to re-visit the marvelous design ingenuity, imagination and sheer styling flair of car body designers in the classic years. In the Twenties and Thirties they had many separate elements with which to cope: the fenders, hood, grille, running boards, lamps, body proper, trunk—which often was literally a trunk—wheels and the elaborate interiors, designed and built to individual order. By comparison designing a modern car is a doddle.

Lennart Haajanen, who knows so well this period and its cars, gives us a look at some wonderful automobiles while recalling the masterful way in which designers in the classic era handled all these elements in a coordinated way to create some of the handsomest automobiles of all time. They present an implicit challenge to the designers of today. Will they do as well to create modern cars that will contribute to the establishment of a heritage of their own? For the sake of future car collectors and enthusiasts, I hope so!

Preface

This dictionary is an attempt to catalog automobile bodywork terms, both contemporary ones and those that automobiles inherited from the horse-drawn carriage era; to list certain automobile model subtype designations; and to clarify why certain terms and designations have been used (or misused).

Many auto bodywork designations have their roots far in the past, often in the age of horse-drawn vehicles. Some of these terms are still used for cars in their original sense, while others have taken on a different meaning and become accepted in their new variation. However, consistency in the use of terms has neither been a strong point with carriage bodywork nor with automobiles; thus, some names have been and are still used merely because they are popular. Others have been applied in order to enhance the product with a designation of high prestige, which the product may not merit, and some have been chosen to meet competition from rival manufacturers. Thus there are no absolutely reliable rules as to what the names imply.

In this work the idea has been to record *automobile terms*—obsolete, old, contemporary and new, with short explanations—and those *carriage terms* which the auto coachbuilding industry and auto manufacturers have inherited from the horse-drawn carriage era. Some odd bodywork detail terms not usually found in works of this kind have been included,

such as *Landau bars* and *Quarter windows.* The entries also encompass a typology of well established model subtype designations—usually abbreviations, such as *GL, GT* and *Ti.*

Greatest in number and importance are the coachbuilding and bodywork designs and terms stemming from France, Italy, the United States, Great Britain and Germany. This dictionary includes terms and expressions in the languages of these countries. However, a number of terms exist only in some of these four languages —or in effect five, as British and American automotive terminology differs markedly. Wherever possible, national specific terms have been pointed out.

Coachbuilding and bodywork nomenclature is the main subject of this work. Nevertheless, since body styles and functional properties in automobiles necessarily overlap, auto models and types as well as certain chassis terms, which affect the bodywork styles, do enter the context. Therefore, special expressions used from time to time to describe a significant body or chassis execution, like *Special* and *Underslung,* are included.

A note about what is meant by "automobile" is necessary. In the United States, in some contexts and statistics Minivans (MPVs) and Sport-utility Vehicles (SUVs) are treated as trucks. Also, in the excellent *Standard Catalog of American Cars 1976–1999* these vehicle types are conspicuous by their absence. Not so in the present dictionary, which endeavors to comprise all normal passenger carrying vehicles smaller than buses. Trucks are excluded.

Many automobile manufacturing companies as well as most coachbuilding firms have had a particular proclivity for giving their products misleading style names; e.g., Brougham to non–Brougham body styles, or unnecessary combinations of well established or fancy terms, e.g. Saloon Coupé Cabriolet for a Coupé Landaulet body and Sedancalette de Ville when Landaulet would suffice. Such terms have quite purposely been avoided in this work. However, complementary information on non-fanciful terms is sought, and the author therefore welcomes additions and corrections, sent in care of the publisher.

This work does not pretend to be complete. It would be presumptuous to think that *all* names, designations and denotations that have been applied to automobile bodywork within the scope of the languages of this work could be included.

Bodywork terms

Quite a few bodywork names that we still use owe their origins to the seventeenth, eighteenth and nineteenth centuries, the period of the horse-drawn vehicle. Indeed, in the beginning the *carrosserie* for automobiles were constructed using well-proven techniques and bodywork styles from the coachbuilding trade. Quite naturally, many early automobile bodyworks were built by the very coachbuilders that had long standing experience and skills in building horse-drawn carriages. Many of the very first and less innovative automobiles were in fact motorized carriages, complete with a driver's perch in front and engine tucked away under the vehicle's framework.

Soon enough, however, the increasing speed of the automobile demanded seating positions that differed from those of the horse-drawn vehicles. It became no longer either safe or practical for the driver—not to mention passengers—to sit at the very front of the car or, as with the Vis-à-vis bodywork, having two passengers facing the rear seat driver.

There was a wide variety of motor driven vehicles for passenger transportation before World War I. At the highest level was the Limousine; initially the driver, like the coachman of the horse-drawn carriage, sat outside, a reflection on the powers of tradition. The Landaulet was a variation, having the rearmost part of the bodywork in the form of a collapsible top. Some of the open Tonneau automobiles from the first years of the 20th century had chain rear-wheel drive which rendered side entry to the rear seats difficult, so the well proven rear central door from the horse-drawn Brake was resorted to. Subsequently propeller shaft drive to a live rear axle enabled side rear doors to be introduced.

Around 1910 automobile speeds had risen to such a high level that external bodywork "streamlining"—hitherto tentatively applied only to cars intended for racing—was adopted for the ordinary automobile. An important bodywork component in this context was the "torpedo bonnet," a bodywork part that closed the gap between the engine hood and the doorless front seat(s). A consequence was that the windscreen, when fitted, could be moved farther back, and in a few years the torpedo hood, or cowl, became contoured and integrated between the engine hood proper and the front driver-cum-passenger compartment.

Terms described in this book are the

singular as well as the basic ones. To define more closely a certain body style of vehicle, a combination of terms may be helpful or sometimes even necessary. A practical case in point was the American way of differentiating between an open two-door and an open four-door auto by specifying Convertible Coupe and Convertible Sedan, respectively.

Some bodywork characteristics are interconnected with chassis characteristics. Therefore you find some designations herein that are perhaps normally associated with an automobile's chassis, or otherwise technically design-orientate.

Few things have been subject to so many confusing type names and designations as automobile models and body styles. An example is "Dorsay," which was used by coachbuilders between the two World Wars inconsistently for all kinds of auto coachwork—Coupés, Berlines, Cabriolets, Touring Cars and others. Another is "Touring," used by a couple of modern manufacturers to denote their Station Wagon models. The automobile industry, being one of the largest in the world, provides work for a great number of people. Today this worldwide industry more than satisfies the need for various types of passenger vehicles. Competition is a matter of life and death for many auto producing enterprises. Manufacturers try to augment their products' attractiveness by using fancy names despite the fact that such denominations are often misleading and sometimes even incorrect. The practice frequently causes confusion.

Model subtype designations

The abundance of subtype designations (type name initials, often with relevance to bodywork) makes a comprehensive listing of such terms difficult. Those that have been included are generally subtype designations used by comparatively many manufacturers, or ones that have reached international acceptance, usually through some very famous past vehicle types or bodywork styles.

Many subtype designations or initials seem to have been applied more to enhance the vehicle for marketing purposes than to define the style of the bodywork or type of product. Most subtype designations therefore do not readily lend themselves to rational explanation; for example "SX" or "RN" (from which the "X" could possibly be construed as "extra"). A number of inquiries to car manufacturers have solicited only two replies and these have been only partly elucidatory. It is significant, though, that a small number of manufacturers are continuously able to market their cars without having to resort to pompous names or fanciful initials.

Explanations

Within entries, bodywork names and terms in italics with *backward pointing arrows* refer to earlier-used terms, predecessor body styles, and origins related to the term in question. *Forward pointing arrows* refer to later terms, additional information or variant terms. A superscript numeral (or numerals), refers to one of several definitions of a term; for example, [3]Brake.

Capitalized terms in the text exist as freestanding entries. These entries will contain more information.

As far as possible the original language term which seems historically to have made the most far-reaching impact is used, with reference made to terms in the languages of other countries.

The approximate period of time of

each bodywork name or term, unless specified within the entry, will be roughly indicated by the accompanying illustration.

The preferred spelling forms in the respective languages, as set out by acknowledged and well known dictionaries, have been followed.

Lennart Haajanen

THE
DICTIONARY

-A-

Aerodinamica

This term is Italian and used to mean "streamlined" generally. In connection with road vehicles, and particularly cars, it means that the external bodywork has a streamlined shape to lessen aerodynamic drag.

→ *Profilé*

Airport Limo/Airport Limousine

An enclosed, comfortable multi-passenger and multi-door chauffeur-driven automobile, also called Stretch-limo, employed by airline companies etc. An earlier vehicle for this purpose was the Parlor Coach.

Origins and history

The Airport or Stretch-limo had its predecessors around World War II when mainly airline companies, but also hotels, found it necessary to transport their customers in nimbler vehicles than regular buses swiftly to and from the airport and other locations. With increasing air traffic and larger airports the need arose for passenger transportation within airport areas as well as between local airline terminals.

²Parlor Coach ←

Important period
1930s–present.

Variations
In the USA, Europe and other countries larger sized vans fitted out with side windows and multiple seating are sometimes employed as Airport Limousines.

They constitute modern and somewhat smaller versions of the pre–1930s Parlor Coaches *(see Passenger Van).* European vehicles corresponding to Airport Limousines are usually lengthened versions of standard Sedan cars.

→ *Stretch-limo*

À la Daumont

A method of driving, and also style name of, the Caleche carriage, *see ²Calèche.*

All-weather/Allweather Touring Car

An open two- or four-door automobile seating four or five and having a folding high-quality soft top, tight-fitting doors, wind-down (sometimes stow-away) glass windows combined with fold-down or removable, typically thick, B-pillars and otherwise very good protection against inclement weather. A high-quality folding mechanism was used to operate both the soft top and windows. In America such a top design was known as a Springfield Top (Walker). A characteristic of the All-weather body was its aptness for

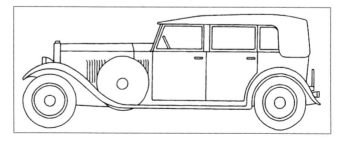

Allweather Touring Car. The thick B-pillar was a characteristic of many Allweather bodies.

travel with the top down and side windows up, thereby in a way anticipating the Sunshine saloon. A comparatively expensive vehicle.

Origins and history

This type of bodywork emerged as an alternative to the normal Touring Car, which provided popular open air motoring but could not offer nearly as effective weather protection as the contemporary, heavy enclosed automobile. Answering the need for a lighter but completely weather-tight touring type of vehicle, the Allweather Touring Car was the precursor of the 1930s Cabriolet/Convertible *(see ³Cabriolet /Convertible)*.

Touring Car ←

Important period

Some years before WWI to the early 1930s.

Variations

In the 1930s USA the term Convertible became widely used for roughly this type of bodywork, consistent with improved tightness, wind-down glass windows, soft top closing mechanisms etc. LaSalle in 1930-31 used the term Allweather Phaeton. The only external difference that could reasonably be detected between an Allweather Touring Car and a Convertible, or an Allweather Phaeton, could be the thick B-pillar of particularly some coach built Allweather Touring cars.

Language varieties

American: All-weather, Allweather Touring Car.

British: All-weather, All-weather Tourer.

French: Voiture Transformable Tous Temps.

German: Transformations-Kabriolett, Allwetter.

Italian: Vettura Trasformabile.

→ *Convertible*; *³Cabriolet*

Allwetter

Alternative German term for All-weather Touring Car.

→ *All-weather*

All Wheel Drive (AWD, awd)

AWD, and the alternatives 4x4 and 4WD *(q.v.)*, are used by some auto manufacturers as subtype designations to indicate four wheel drive (applicable to vehicles with four road wheels). Four-by-four is a variant. An earlier term was FWD which is no longer used, and should not be confused with an American heavy vehicle manufacturer using these initials in its company name. It should be noted that AWD implies that all road wheels are driven irrespective of the number of road wheels. Thus, "all wheel drive" could also be used to indicate that more than four wheels are driven, e.g. all six wheels in a vehicle having six wheels (6x6), all eight in an eight-wheeled vehicle (8x8) etc.

→ *Off-roader*

All-year Top

A complete greenhouse appendage with windowed upper half doors, wind-

All-year top. The detachable top to convert a Touring Car to a Sedan was an idea around World War I that did not quite catch on.

3 1833 05387 9802

shield and rear view window to fit onto an open automobile body to make it enclosed. In mainly the 1920s, a small number of car manufacturers and coachbuilders in the USA as well as in Europe offered detachable "All-year" tops for their Touring and two- and three-seater Roadster cars. These tops were provided with links and locks for fastening to the main body and connecting the framed and hinged windows to the doors, thereby transforming the open car into a Sedan or Coupe, as the case might be. Kissel Motor Car Co. was the prominent American exponent of the All-year top, offering both Sedan and Coupe tops from 1914 to 1919. California Top was a curious alternative name, as shelter for bad weather is not the first thing that comes to mind with regard to California. Detachable and All-year are other alternative designations. A post–World War II near counterpart was the removable Hardtop.

Important period
1910–1930
→ *²Hardtop*

¹Ambulance

French term for a provisional (ambulant) medical establishment.

²Ambulance

A vehicle specially equipped for transporting sick or injured people on stretcher(s) or similar.

Origins and history

The first ambulances were horse-drawn carts used in 1797 during Napoleon I's military campaign on Italy. Motorized ambulances began to be used around 1900 and were generally based on production automobile chassis. Today, ambulances are efficient, purpose-built vehicles.

Language varieties

American: Ambulance.
British: Ambulance.
French: Ambulance.
German: Ambulanz.
Italian: Ambulanza, Autoambulanza.

Ambulanz

German for Ambulance.
→ *²Ambulance*

Ambulanza

Italian for Ambulance.
→ *²Ambulance*

Americaine

A French, light four-wheeled carriage constructed on the lines of American Buggies.
Buggy ←

Amphibian, Amphibian vehicle

Vehicle designed to move on land and in water. All kinds of permutations have been produced over a large number of years—open bodywork, enclosed bodywork, civilian, military, screw propelled, road wheel propelled, etc.

Language varieties

American: Amphibian.
British: Amphibian.
French: Véhicule amphibie.
German: Amphibienfahrzeug.
Italian: Veicolo anfibio.

Amphibienfahrzeug

German for Amphibian vehicle.
→ *Amphibian vehicle*

Aperto

Contemporary, informal and loosely used Italian term to denote an open car of unspecified type.
→ *Open Car*
Cabriolet ←

A tetto apribile

Short for Berlina a tetto apribile. Italian for "with Sunroof."
→ *Sunshine Saloon*

A tetto rigido

Short for Vettura a tetto rigido. Italian alternative for Hardtop.
→ *[1]Hardtop*

Auto

1. German short for Automobil. Alternative to the colloquial Wagen. *See also Personenkraftwagen.*
2. French short for Automobile. Colloquial alternative to Voiture *(q.v.).*
3. Italian short for Autovettura. Alternative to the colloquial Macchina. *See also Automobile.*
→ *[6]Car*

Autoambulanza

Italian alternative for Ambulanza.
→ *[2]Ambulance*

Autobahn Kurier

German for Gran Turismo.
→ *Gran Turismo*

Auto-buggy

Alternative name for Buggy. An American very early, light, open two-seater motor propelled vehicle on high and slim wheels, rather similar to its horse-drawn counterpart. For weather protection usually only a Victoria-type folding top. *See also High-wheeler.*
[2]Buggy ←

Automobile

The *Motoring Encyclopedia & Touring Gazetteer* of 1934 says under this heading:
"Originally meaning self-moving in a general sense, this term has by custom been limited in its application to mechanical propelled vehicles of the private passenger type. In Great Britain the terms motor car, motor or car are more generally used; but in North America the term automobile or its contraction, auto, is always used."

Automobile is still the formal term for car in North American and British English, French and Italian. However, the pronunciation between these three differ considerably.
→ *[6]Car*

Automobile di piazza

Italian (obsolete) for Taxi. The name derives from the fact that in the early days vehicles for hire used to have their cabstand at the open market places, or piazzas.
→ *[2]Cab; Taxi*
[2]Fiacre ←

Autotelaio

Italian for Chassis.
→ *Chassis*

Autovettura

Formal Italian term for car. Alternative to Automobile.
→ *[6]Car*

Avant-train

A two-wheeled power unit consisting of engine, gearbox, final drive, steering wheel and other controls, which could replace a horse-drawn vehicle's front axle or be applied to other kinds of bodies/chassis. Bodywork design was not one of the outstanding features of these conveyances. Avant-train units were the earliest examples of front-wheel drive, but were outmoded after 1900. Electric as well as gasoline engines were used (*Beaulieu Encyclopædia of the Automobile*). Automobile Fore Carriage of New

York produced such a unit around 1900. Apparently, carriage-style simple, single pivot steering was employed.

AWD, awd
Abbreviation of All Wheel Drive
→ *All-wheel Drive*

-B-

Barchetta
Italian for an open, small *pukka (q.v.)* two-seater Sports Car essentially with full-width bodywork and no soft or hard top at all for weather protection. It could be contended that the Barchetta is a modern full-width version of an early Runabout or Spider.

Origins and history
Barchetta is a comparatively late bodywork term. The first Barchettas seem to have been designed by Ferrari soon after World War II. Barchetta is a diminutive form of the Italian "barca," meaning a small vessel or skiff. (The correct Italian pronunciation is "barketta.")

Important period
This bodywork style has been produced sporadically since its initiation in the late 1940s. As recently as the 1990s Fiat revived the name in their Punto-based sporting car.

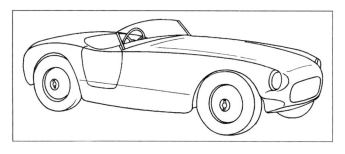

Barchetta. The "little boat" nomenclature seems to have come from the all-enveloping bodywork and boat-like cockpit of this style of Sports Car.

Language varieties
French: Barquette.
→ *⁴Spider; Pukka; ¹, ²Sports car*

¹Barouche
American and British term for Caleche; i.e., an open four-wheeled, elegant, horse-drawn carriage with two transverse passenger seats facing each other. The two-door body for four passengers is, depending on period of production, leather-brace suspended on C-springs or fully elliptic steel springs. It has a folding top over the rear seats only. For the coachman and footman in front there is a raised open perch with a back-rest. For illustration, *see Calèche.*

Origins and history
This carriage type came to England from Germany in the 1760s, and it has been contended that it was initially referred to as "the German carriage." The origins of the term Barouche go back to an early period when the vehicle was still a two-wheeled carriage. The name can be traced via the German Barutsche and Italian biroccio/baroccio to "birotus," Latin for two-wheeled. It is not clear why the name Barouche became adopted by the English.

¹Calèche
Important period
19th century.
Variations
The coachman's seat in front could be removed in order to drive the Barouche by postilions, à la Daumont style—*see ²Calèche.*
Language varieties
After an initial period, the term Calèche, according to Robert Sallmann, was in 19th century England "little used." Although definitely a term adopted by the British, László Tarr in his work refers to the name Barouche as being popular in France. The automobile term derivation, the Landaulet, can be traced via the horse-drawn Calèche and the Landau.
> *American*: Barouche.
> *British*: Barouche.
> *French*: Calèche.
> *German*: Kalesche.
> *Italian*: Calèsse or Calèche.

²Barouche

According to The Classic Car Club of America, Barouche was "very rarely used for automobiles. The driver sat in an open front seat with two couples facing each other inside a closed cabin. There was a folding top over the rear seat." The folding top over the rear seat only would indicate a very early motor vehicle modeled after the horse-drawn carriage described above.

Barquette

French for Barchetta *(q.v.)*.

Bateau

A sporting, usually open, automobile with a pointed Boattail bodywork style. This French name was often rendered as Torpédo Bateau or Voiture de tourisme Bateau to encompass the whole vehicle.
Origins and history
The name originated with the pointed boat style tail. From time to time style and materials from the sailing boat hull were adopted, mostly by coachbuilders, for car bodywork. In particular, the tail treatment lent itself well to be transposed into the bodywork of the open post–World War I car.
Important period
1920s and 1930s.
Variations
The Bateau tail is a French and Italian alternative to Skiff. (To be strict, the Skiff tail is rounded, not pointed.)
→ *Boattail; Bordino; Skiff*

Beach Buggy

A light, simple and open, two- or four-wheel driven vehicle with large low-pressure tyres for traveling on sand and having originally some utilitarian purposes.
Origins and history
These vehicles probably originated before World War II. They are known to have been used in the United States by East Coast fishing people, later to become vehicles for sport and leisure.
Important period
Late 1930s to present.
Variations
Beach Buggy should not be confused with Dune Buggy. The Dune Buggy, although having some similar characteristics, was not really a variation of Beach Buggy but a separate kind of vehicle for leisure purposes on beach sand. The original Buggy was an American light horse-drawn carriage, precursor of the motorized vehicle by the same denomination. The term Beach Buggy is internationally known and used.
→ *Dune Buggy*

Beach Wagon

A Station Wagon type of motor vehicle with wooden body to accommodate at least seven people.

Origins and history

These vehicles originated in New England, probably before World War II, and were used to transport families on holiday in summertime to and from the beach — the car filled with children, umbrellas, picnic baskets etc. (Andy Rheault).
→ Station Wagon

[1]Berlina

Italian for an 18th century horse-drawn, four-wheeled, fully suspended, enclosed traveling coach having a raised seat outside in front for the coachman. Four passengers had two-seat benches facing each other.
[1]Berline ←

[2]Berlina

Contemporary Italian for an owner-driven Sedan bodied fours- or five-seater, usually four-door, enclosed car. For illustration, see [3]Berline.
→ [4]Sedan
[1]Berlina; [3]Berline ←

Berlina 3-porte

Italian for Hatchback Coupe.
→ Hatchback Coupe

Berlina 5-porte

Italian for Hatchback Sedan.
→ Hatchback Sedan

Berlina allungata

Italian for a Stretch-limo with division glass behind the driver's compartment.
→ Stretch-limo

Berlina a tetto apribile

Italian for a Sedan with Sunroof.
→ Sunshine Saloon

Berlina da Viaggio

Italian for Berline de Voyage.
→ Berline de Voyage

Berlina Guida interna

Italian for a chauffeur driven Limousine style automobile with a glass division separating the passenger compartment from the chauffeur.
→ [2]Limousine

Berlina Sport

Italian for a sporting Sedan.
→ Sports Saloon

[1]Berline

French and German for an early horse-drawn, leather-brace suspended four-wheeled traveling carriage for four passengers. The passenger compartment had two seat benches facing each other. A raised outside seat in front was provided for the coachman. Early carriages were initially open with a folding top, whereas the traditional Berline was enclosed and generally known as such. The Berline was one of the most important vehicles of the horse-drawn era.

Origins and history

It has been assumed, according to Sallmann and earlier research, that it was the Sovereign of Brandenburg in Germany, Friedrich Wilhelm, who had his General quartermaster Philippe de Chiese commission around 1660 the construction of a new type of carriage for a journey from Berlin to Paris. The novelty lay in the design of the undercarriage which utilized *twin* booms, or brancards, instead of the single one that had hitherto been the norm for undercarriages of horse-drawn vehicles. This traveling carriage received considerable attention in Paris, and was in France thenceforth called "la berline." The

[1]Berline. The 3/4-elliptic rear suspension of this Berline carriage enabled the body to retain its Dorsay back form (see d'Orsay, Dorsay)

the 17th century the good design and comfortable ride of the Berline carriages made them take over the role of the traditional, heavy and luxurious State and Gala Coaches.

Carozza; [1]*Coach* ←

Important period

Second half of 17th through 19th century.

Variations

Some of the later German Berline town carriages were built with the front part of the body cut off so as to accommodate two forward facing passengers only. This carriage style was termed in German Halbberline ("half-Berline") and constituted the basis for the Berline automobile. Also in France a smaller Berline carriage variation with seating for two was built, at first called Berlingot or Berline Coupé (from the French verb *couper* meaning cut), later just Coupé.

→ *Berlingot;* [1]*Coupé*

Language varieties

The Berline type of carriage became widely used in Continental Europe, as did the originally French term in other languages—some with slight spelling variations.

Whereas Berline or Berlin in the meaning of a carriage does not appear in British dictionaries, the American Webster of 1937 specifies Berlin as "a four-wheel carriage with covered seat behind, separate from the body" and Webster 1979 says "a four-wheeled two-seated covered carriage with a hooded rear seat." However, as in Great Britain, Coach would be the nearest American equivalent to the carriage type under consideration. In Great Britain the

most recent research (Rudolf H. Wackernagel via Sallman) indicates, however, that there already existed in France utilitarian horse-drawn goods wagons incorporating a twin-boomed undercarriage design similar to the Chiesecarriage, but that the appearance of the new German passenger carriage in Paris influenced the French to commence building elegant but durable twin-boom traveling and shooting carriages as well. Originally, in German Prussia, the body of this type of carriage was designed open with a collapsible top, but it was later built and established—no doubt due to the notoriously bad weather conditions in that region—as an enclosed type of carriage. Later Berline carriages in France underwent further technical improvements to undercarriage design which made the twin-boom undercarriage not always obligatory. Therefore, the term Berline, having been initially applied to passenger carriages using the new undercarriage design, took on in the 18th century the general meaning of an enclosed and elegant carriage for town use, and in more luxurious form also for formal and ceremonial functions. Thus, starting in

Double Brougham was also a designation for a corresponding carriage.

American: Coach.
British: Coach, Double Brougham.
French: Berline
German: Berline.
Italian: Berlina.

²Berline

The first Berline automobiles had a two-door closed compartment for four passengers facing each other, the two front ones on occasional seats. The driver's (and footman's) seat was external, in front of the passenger compartment. The Berline body style was basically similar to the early Coupé automobile. For illustration, see ²Coupé.

Origins and history

After the first approximately two decades of experimental and crude self-propelled motor cars it became generally accepted to locate the internal combustion engine at the front, in fact more or less in the place previously taken by the horse or horses. Otherwise, compared to the Halbberline carriage, there was little change. The chauffeur and his controls were merely brought down to the level of the passengers, but remained in the open, and the enclosed passenger compartment body was adapted to the automobile chassis. The name of the Berline automobile derives of course from the horse-drawn carriage. (It is interesting that the old city name Berlin, meaning "swamp" in the ancient Sorbian language, has been widely used outside Germany as a carriage and eventually an automobile body style term.)

¹Berline ←
Important period
From the first decade of the 20th century up to World War I.
Variations
Later, when the chauffeur was provided with a permanent roof and full enclosure, the car was still for some time termed Berline. This term was later captured by the owner-driver family car *(see ³Berline)*, whereas the chauffeur-driven variation became for all intents and purposes the Limousine *(q.v.)*.
→ *²Coupé*
Language varieties
Although in fact a motorized Halbberline, the German term for this automobile was initially just Berline, later in the period changing to Kupee/Coupé to align with the internationally accepted French Coupé.

³Berline

The term Berline became subsequently established in French speaking countries as the normal name for an enclosed non–chauffeur driven four-door vehicle for four to six passengers, driver included, having four or six side windows, the rearmost usually being small. In other words, a Sedan car.

³Berline. The old Berline name lives on in European Sedans.

Origins and history

The Berline name was applied to enclosed owner-driver Sedan cars, initially and to be entirely strict, to the two-door variation with four side windows (four-light) only. Later it was applied also to four-door and four to six side-windowed cars when chauffeur-driven vehicles became too expensive and rare and mass production cars became available to the owner-driver, for family or business use.

²*Berline* ←

Important period

The importance of the non-chauffeur driven Berline car manifested itself after World War I and has remained so—with variations to the basic bodywork style—into modern times.

Variations

The earliest use of the Berline epithet by an American automobile manufacturer appears to have been by Locomobile, starting in 1912. Thereafter, a handful of manufacturers, but perhaps more so coachbuilding companies, applied the designation (somewhat inconsistently) to their products between 1916 and 1940. Somewhat strangely, the American car manufacturers in the 1930s tended to apply the term to large, seven passenger Limousines, whereas late 1920s custom built elaborately appointed four or five passenger four-door, four-windowed vehicles were called Sedans.

Language varieties

American: Sedan.
British: Saloon.
French: Berline
German: Limousine, but also Berline, which is to-day a rather rare German term.
Italian: Berlina.
→ ³,⁴*Sedan; Conduite intérieure;*
³*Coach*

Berline à 3 portes.

French for Hatchback Coupe.
→ *Hatchback Coupe*

Berline à 5 portes.

French for Hatchback Sedan.
→ *Hatchback Sedan*

Berline Cabriolet

French (arch.) for a four-door Convertible car.
→ ³*Cabriolet*

Berline Coupé

The first name for a small horse-drawn Berline carriage for just two passengers was Berlingot, alternatively Berlin Coupé. Later, Berlin Coupé became abbreviated to just Coupé.
→ ¹*Coupé*
¹*Berline* ←

Berline de Voyage

A heavy automobile with bodywork suitable for long distance travel, the illustrated specimen emulating styling features of horse-drawn carriage bodies and having a large, fixed roof rack for carrying luggage. An enclosed compartment held up to five passengers. The chauffeur originally had no weather protection but soon received a windshield, a canopy roof and doors and eventually full enclosure. The foldable little hood in front of the windshield as illustrated was for protecting the windshield from rain.

Origins and history

The Berline de Voyage was a development of the early Berline automobile.
²*Berline* ←

Important period
1905–1915.

Variations
The chauffeurs of Berline de Voyage

Berline de Voyage. An early form of Touring Limousine.

automobiles produced during the last years before World War I were provided with full enclosure. Some specimens were produced with a Landaulet-type rear Quarter folding top. A few automobiles made between the World Wars were given model names to associate with travel, but were really no different from the standard Limousine or Sedan.

Language varieties
American: Touring Limousine.
British: Touring Limousine.
French: Berline de Voyage.
German: Reise-Limousine.
Italian: Berlina da Viaggio.
➡ *Touring Limousine*

Berline quatre places rapprochées

French for Close-coupled Sedan.
➡ *Close-coupled; ³Coach*

Berline Sport

French for Sports Saloon.
➡ *Sports Saloon*

Berlinetta

Italian for, strictly, a small two-door post–World War II Berlina

(Sedan), generally similar in style to the Berlina. The Berlinetta term, which is a diminutive form of Berlina, has been applied to small closed two-door, close-coupled Four-light four-seaters, usually with a Fastback or slant-back type of bodywork, but also, somewhat illogically, to obvious Coupé style bodywork. The two rear seats are generally less comfortable than the front ones.

Variations
An earlier American vehicle style, but in relative size almost comparable, was the Coach *(see ²Coach)*. The term Berlinetta has often been applied by manufacturers, especially outside Italy and not quite appropriately, to Two-plus-two or even two-seater Coupé bodywork styles. Although Berlinetta is an internationally known designation its application is muddled.

Language varieties
Except for the French term version Berlinette, other languages lack a precisely corresponding body style term.
American: Coach or Close-coupled Sedan.

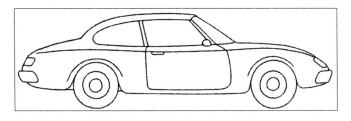

Berlinetta. This name means literally "small Berline" but has been applied to some Coupé bodywork styles as well.

British: Close-coupled Saloon.
French: Berlinette.
German: Limousine, 4 Sitze.
Italian: Berlinetta.
→ *Close-coupled Sedan*
Demi-berline ←

Berlinette

French for Berlinetta. A two-door small enclosed post–World War II French Berline body style. An earlier French term for a basically almost similar but older style of bodywork was the Coach. The Coach body style was preceded around World War I by the Demi-berline. The contemporary European Coupé body with capacity for four passengers (*⁴Coupé*) would gain from being termed Berlinette or Berlinetta.
→ *Berlinetta; ³Coach*
Demi-berline ←

Berlingot

A French term (arch.) for one of the first horse-drawn small Coupé carriages with seating for two passengers and designed on a 17th century style Berline undercarriage. The name Berlingot probably derived from Berline (Sallman). Later the term Coupé became widely used.
→ *¹Coupé*
¹Berline ←

Bestattungswagen

German for Hearse.
→ *Hearse*

Bicorps

French alternative way to describe a Two-box or Fastback bodywork style.
→ *Fastback*

Biga

Italian for a two-wheeled war and racing Chariot.
→ *Chariot*

Boattail, Boat-tail

This refers to the style and line of the rear bodywork portion of an open or, sometimes, enclosed bodywork style. The light, open version was usually a three-seater car with the single rear seat centrally located, cloverleaf style. Touring Cars, Sports Tourers and Sports Cars were also quite often subject to the Boattail rear end treatment in various forms. As is the case with many other body style terms, although Boattail refers only to part of the body, often the designation is combined with another body style name to render the description more precise. A case in point would the Torpédo Bateau. Boattail alone has also, colloquially, been used to denote the complete car, not only the bodywork style. The classic American Speedster is a prime example of the Boattail bodywork style; *see Speedster*.

Origins and history

From time to time styles and materials from the sailing boat hull have been adopted, mostly by coachbuilders, for car bodywork. In particular the boat stern, and sometimes the bow, lent themselves well to be transposed into the bodywork of the open post–World War I car.

Important period
1920s and 1930s

Variations

The Boattail is usually pointed but sometimes rendered rounded. The French use different terms for these variations: the pointed tail is called Bateau, whereas the rounded one is Skiff. Bordino is an Italian bodywork style in

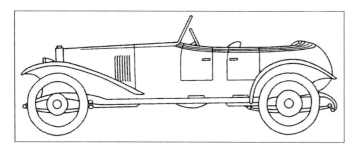

Boattail. A style name applied to bodyworks, usually to Touring Cars, having a boat-like posterior.

which the tail terminates in a vertical tip.

Language varieties
Bateau and Fish-tail are alternatives to Boattail. Boattail/Boat-tail seems to have been favored by Anglo-Americans.
American: Boattail.
British: Boat-tail.
French: Bateau, Skiff, Pointe Bateau.
German: Bootsheck.
Italian: Bateau, Coda Bateau.
➝ *Bateau; Bordino; Skiff*

Bodywork
1. The design and process of manufacturing the external shell for a motor vehicle.
2. The external shell of a motor vehicle.
Language varieties
American and British: Coachwork, Bodywork.
French: Carrosserie.
German: Karosserie.
Italian: Carrozzeria.
➝ *Coachwork*

Bootsheck
German for Boat-tail.
➝ *Boattail*

Bordino
A pointed rearmost automobile body part, terminating in a vertical tip.
Origins and history
Pietro Bordino was one of the successful racing drivers of the early 1920s, working for Fiat. Tracing its origins to the beautiful pointed-tail Fiat racing cars, the bodywork name Bordino was used by French and Italian car manufacturers and coachbuilders for a number of open, pointed-tail sporting vehicles, including Sports Tourers, Sports Cars and Racing Cars.
Important period
1920–1940.

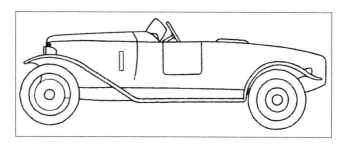

Bordino. A tail form of various Sports and Race cars, mainly in the 1920s.

Language varieties
French: Bordino, Pointe Bordino.
Italian: Bordino, Coda Bordino.

Box
Box is used in some countries to signify one or several of the main divisions of a car's bodywork. The first Box is the (usually forward) engine compartment, the second is the driver's and passengers' compartment, and the third is the (usually rear) luggage compartment.

The classic Notchback Sedan can be referred to as a Three-box car, whereas some cars lack distinct separations between some of the structures. Thus, a Fastback bodywork could be referred to as a Two-box car.

²Brake. The 19th century Brake's main purpose was to break-in horses, but it could also be used to transport goods.

Language varieties

In Germany Box is used as an internal term in the automobile manufacturing industry rather than by the general public. In Italy and France a Minivan is called Monovolume on account of its lack of several Boxes.

American: Box.
British: Box.
French: Volume or Corps.
German: Box (see above).
Italian: Volume.

→ *Fastback; Greenhouse; Notchback*

¹Brake

A horse-drawn four-wheeled vehicle. A reference from 1609, "A frame to hold anything steady," explains the original meaning of brake: to restrain or limit something from moving about. *Webster's Superior Dictionary* from 1937 (USA) defines Brake as e.g. "A frame for confining refractory horses while shoeing."

²Brake

In about 1830 the term was applied to a heavy open horse-drawn carriage. The vehicle had a high driver's seat in front and a platform undercarriage which could be used for carrying goods. This vehicle was also used for breaking-in young horses.

Language varieties

An alternative term for this early vehicle was Skeleton Brake.

American: Brake.
British: Brake.
French: Breack (arch.), Break d'ecurie.
German: Break, Dressurwagen.
Italian: Breack (arch.), Break.

→ *¹Break*

³Brake

An open horse-drawn vehicle equipped with longitudinal and usually removable seats to carry up to fourteen passengers. Entry was through a rear door and step. A large variety of Brakes or Breaks have been built in diverse countries at different times and they have also been given varying names. A common feature of all is a fairly heavy type of construction which necessitated at least twin horses to draw. Later, in the second half of the 19th century the term Wagonette came into use to denote a lighter horse-drawn carriage for passengers and light goods transportation.

→ *¹Wagonette*

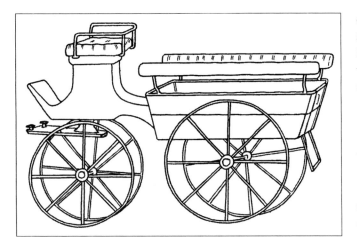

³Brake. The early Brake was designed to enable passengers to be carried.

⁴Brake

With the introduction of automobiles the need to carry passengers was taken over by early open motor propelled vehicles with seating for several persons behind the driver on either longitudinal or transverse seats. Passenger entry was through a central rear door. In enclosed form this type of vehicle was called a Brake (the old spelling of Break) and in practical terms it was the precursor of the Omnibus.

³Brake ←

Important period
End of the 19th century to 1910.

Variations
Although not generally known in the USA as a motorized vehicle, two American manufacturers are known to have constructed around the turn of the previous century English style Brakes, having two or three rows of transverse seats. Char à bancs is the corresponding French type of vehicle. The term Charabanc *(q.v.)* has indeed also been alternatively and frequently used in English parlance. A variation of it, called Shooting Brake, has facilities for carrying passengers and shooting equipment plus sporting dogs.

Language varieties
American: Brake.
British: Brake.
French: Char à bancs.
German: Break.
Italian: Break.
→ *²Break; Shooting Brake*

Breack

Obsolete Italian and French spelling of Break.
→ *¹Break*

¹Break

Non-US variant spelling of a heavy

⁴Brake. The motorized passenger-carrying Brake became in effect an early Omnibus.

horse-drawn open driving vehicle, like *²Brake* above.

²Break

An early car, similar in many ways to the horse-drawn Brake *(³Brake)* and not unlike a large Wagonette.

Language varieties
American: Brake.
British: Break.
French: Char à bancs.
German: Break.
Italian: Break.
→ *²Wagonette*

³Break

British alternative name for a (large) Station Wagon.

⁴Break

French term for a Station Wagon with seating usually limited to six. (A French later period Station Wagon with seating in excess of six was normally termed Familiale.)
→ *Station Wagon*

Break de chasse

French for Shooting Brake.
→ *Shooting Brake*

Break d'écurie

French for Brake.
→ *²Brake*

Brouette

The Brouette is a development of the Sedan chair; in effect a Sedan chair on wheels drawn by one man. The term derives from a Latin term meaning "two small wheels" and is originally French for a small cart pushed or drawn by hand.
²Sedan ←

Brouette. The Brouette sprang from the Sedan chair—a vehicle for one passenger.

¹Brougham

A British elegant four-wheeled, one-horse two-door 19th century light Coupé type of carriage for one or two to three passengers in an enclosed passenger compartment. The body had glass windows in two doors (one each side), and a glass front and panel rear Quarter. The coachman sat on a raised outside seat in front. Features of this body style were threefold: the sharp rear roof termination, the front base body line curving forward (and the front toe of the doors sometimes, but not commonly, following the body line) and the low entry requiring only one outside footstep below the door. In the early days it was not uncommon to have two sets of road wheels—one rubber-tired for town use and one steel-tired set for gravel roads.

Origins and history

Lord Brougham must have found the Clarence a heavy and cumbersome carriage, for in 1838 or 1839 he commissioned the first example of the Brougham carriage to be built by Robinson & Cook, London, to his ideas. The design

¹Brougham. The horse-drawn Brougham was a British opposite number of the French Coupé.

was very successful and proved subsequently most popular with gentlemen about town, civil servants and businessmen. By the late 19th century the small Single Brougham was one of the most common vehicles in English cities (Parry).

Clarence ←

Important period
1840 to ca. 1930.

Variations

Broughams were manufactured in a wide variety during a long period of time. There were Single Broughams (French Coupé Simple) for two passengers, D- or bow-fronted Broughams for three passengers and Double Broughams for four passengers. The horse-drawn Brougham offers many points of comparison with the bodywork of the early similarly named automobile.

²Brougham

Anglo-American variation of

the basically Town Car/Coupé de Ville body style which, in its most correct form, perpetuated the horse-drawn Brougham bodywork characteristics of forward pointing bottom corners (applied to the chauffeur's or passengers' compartment, or both) and sharp rear termination of the roof. The enclosed passenger compartment had capacity for two or three passengers, sometimes with foldable extra seats. In front of the glass division the chauffeur's seat is in the open with the possibility to pull forward or affix a canopy. Later, when the chauffeur was allowed the complete comfort of enclosure, the vehicle (still with a glass division) became a Limousine.

Origins and history

The Brougham originated in England as a horse-drawn vehicle. This style of vehicle was the prerogative of wealthy people, and was therefore—particularly in the beginning of the important pe-

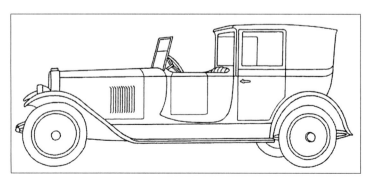

²Brougham. A Coupé de Ville in Anglo-American guise. This illustration shows the shorter passenger compartment of the Single Brouham.

riod and especially with regard to the typical Brougham bodywork features—exclusively built by specialist coachbuilders.

¹Brougham ←

Important period
1910 to 1930.

Variations
A larger style of Brougham, characterized by having a more spacious passenger compartment, usually with two side windows each side and seating for five or six passengers, is a Limousine Brougham. A Brougham automobile having the facility of completely enclosing the chauffeur's compartment was sometimes by coachbuilders specified as Transformable Brougham.

Language varieties
Town Car was a somewhat later term in America for an automobile built for the same purpose, but with a body style that did not display the features that characterized the Brougham. It would appear that Continental coachbuilders did not distinguish between the Brougham body style and the traditional Coupé de Ville.

American: Brougham.

British: Brougham.

French and international: Coupé de Ville.

German: Stadt-Limousine.

Italian: Coupé di città, Coupé de Ville.

→ *Coupé de Ville*

³Brougham

An early electric automobile, either chauffeur-driven, Brougham style as above, with an enclosed passenger compartment, or inside drive. Later, around 1920, most enclosed electric cars were Coach-like owner-driver vehicles, but still designated Brougham *(see Electric Brougham)*. It would seem apparent that the enclosed cars after the 1920s (mentioned below) inherited the Brougham designation from these electric vehicles.

→ *Electric Brougham*

²Brougham ←

⁴Brougham

In America, starting in the 1920s Brougham became a popular bodywork designation applied variously up to approximately World War II by automobile manufacturers to inside drive, short roofed two- or four-door enclosed bodies, where the name appears to have had the purpose of indicating an up-market trim level, thus enhancing the desirability of the model. The illustrated early 1920s vehicle exhibits the last trace of the original Brougham body features in the form of a sharp top rear roof contour. With Opera-style rear Quarter windows and dummy Landau bars the vehicles became even more prestigious. The ancestry could reasonably be traced via the early outside drive Electric

⁴Brougham. An early 1920s American Brougham automobile body style.

Broughams which subsequently became inside drive cars. After World War II, until the mid–1980s, Brougham was applied as a model or trade name to some top-of-the-line—externally more or less normal looking but reputedly handbuilt—Sedan-style cars. Even some elegant Convertible bodyworks were quite improperly designated Brougham without having any affinity at all to that time-honored name.

[3]*Brougham* ⟵

Bubblecar

Term used to describe a very small, mostly European, immediately post–World War II Microcar most of which were Three-wheelers.

German: Kabinenroller.

→ *Microcar; Tricar*

[1]**Buggy**

American important early light, two- or four-seater four-wheeled horse-drawn open carriage characterized by strong and slender, very large diameter wheels made of hickory, and by half- or full-elliptic steel spring suspension systems.

Origins and history

The history of the Buggy carriage, as explained by Sallmann, has not been satisfactorily elucidated, but goes a long way back. It is known that the English single-horse-drawn Buggy was described from 1770 as a light single- or two-seater, two-wheeled carriage without a top. Later versions were four-wheelers. According to Tarr, the American Buggy series produced from 1826 on owed its light design more to French models than to the heavier English ones, and was renowned for its durability and superior quality. In fact, it has been contended by some historians that the name Buggy originated in France.

Important period

18th and 19th centuries.

Variations

French dictionaries vary in the spelling of the name and in the description of the carriages built in France. Buggy could well derive from Boghei or Boguet, which are French designations for a two-wheeled carriage employing very long and thin booms. A later French kind of Buggy, built on the lines of the American one, was in France called Americaine. The term Buggy became also used in German, and one variation, mentioned in 1870, employed back-to-back seating.

[2]**Buggy**

An American very early, light, open two-seater motor propelled

[1]**Buggy. The horse-drawn light Buggy was the forerunner of the American Buggy and High-wheeler automobiles.**

vehicle on high and slim wheels, rather similar to its horse-drawn counterpart as above. For weather protection at most only a Victoria-type folding top. *See High-wheeler.*

[1]Buggy ←

[3]Buggy

Abbreviation for Dune Buggy.

→ *Dune Buggy*

Business Coupe

An American car having a small two/three-passenger Coupe body and good facilities for carrying the traveling salesman's samples and effects in the trunk and, therefore, having no Rumble seat. The differences between the Business Coupe and other Coupe models, like the standard Coupe and Club Coupe, are mainly the simpler rendition and the lower retail price. *See also [3]Coupe.*

Important period
Late 1920s to late 1950s.

[3]Coupé ←

Business Sedan

According to factory records, some American enclosed two- and four-door vehicles termed Business Sedan have been manufactured periodically in some surprising varieties: as three-, five-, eight- and nine-seaters. Little information can be found about them, but the suspicion is that the two-door, three passenger vehicle was in fact a Business Coupe rendered as Sedan in the factory records (which have therefore been treated with some reservation as regards model names). The four-door, eight- and nine-passenger bodied Business Sedans could be assumed to have been cars particularly directed towards company use. In subsequent years one of the manufacturers recorded this size of vehicle as Imperial Sedan. The Business Sedan in all its rare permutations was probably a cheaper version of the makers' corresponding normal product, the Sedan.

Important period
Mid–1940s to early 1960s.

[3, 4]Sedan ←

Bustleback

American colloquial expression for a Notchback style bodywork, usually a Sedan. According to *Webster's New Collegiate Dictionary* of 1979, a third alternative meaning of bustle is "a pad or framework expanding and supporting the fullness and drapery of the back of a woman's skirt," which makes good sense of the use of Bustleback for Notchback.

→ *Notchback*

-C-

C

This sub-type designation has been employed variously and during different periods of time by car manufacturers to indicate Cabriolet, Competition/Com-pétition/ Competizione, Cylinder, Corto (Italian for short), Court (French for short) or Coupé, as the case may be.

One of the most recent additions using the letter C was introduced in the fall of 2000 when Peugeot re-introduced their folding hard top model 206 CC, the twin letters standing for Coupé Cabriolet *(q.v.)*.

¹Cab

A horse-drawn carriage used for public hire, initially constructed on the lines of the Cabriolet carriage. Subsequently, the British Cabriolet-type carriage was developed and refined into the purpose-built Hansom Cab, variations of which existed in many countries.
→ *Hansom Cab*
¹Cabriolet ←

²Cab

Anglo-American for a horseless vehicle used for public hire; i.e., a taxi. Also in France, in the transition period when the horse-drawn Cab became motor-propelled, this term was used by the French for both variations.
→ *Taxi*
¹Cab ←

³Cab

Short for cabin; i.e., the enclosed driving compartment of a lorry, truck, locomotive or crane.

Cabrio

Contemporary German informal term to denote an "open car" of unspecified type. It is not uncommon in Germany and German speaking countries, however, for Cabrio, which derives from Cabriolet, to mean a sporting type car.
→ *Open Car*
Cabriolet ←

Cabrio-Coach

Alternative and apparently obsolete term used in some European countries,

among them the Nordic and Swiss, for a normally two-door Sunroof style of bodywork.

Origins and history
The origins of this combination of terms are somewhat unclear. The Cabrio part obviously derives from the Cabriolet *(see Cabrio-Limousine),* whereas Coach is a fairly widely established vehicle term *(²,³Coach)* without any connotations of the Sunroof facility.

Important period
Ca. 1930 to just after World War II.
→ *Sunroof*

¹Cabriolet

A two-wheeled, suspended one-horse carriage with seating for two persons, a folding hood and usually a platform at the rear for a servant or groom. For private use in town and for short journeys. Normally driven from one of the two seats.

Origins and history
The term Cabriolet can be traced via Italian for goat, *capra,* to the leap of a goat in French, *cabrioler,* and thence to the equestrian *caper.* According to Parry the French *cabriole* is a reference to the smooth, springy motion of the vehicle. Another theory maintains, however, that the folding and unfolding of a soft top resembled the *capriole,* a vertical leap with a backward kick of the hind legs of a trained horse in high school dressage. The Cabriolet carriage was originally a French design which became widely imitated and used in other European countries.

Important period
Nineteenth century.

Variations
A Cabriolet variation became also used for public hire, when it was driven from the rear platform (Garnier).
→ *Hansom Cab*

[1]Cabriolet. This horse-drawn vehicle's name is one of few still current as automobile body style terms.

Language varieties

When used for public hire the British term became Cab, which led to the British purpose-built Hansom Cab.

[2]Cabriolet

An early chauffeur-driven automobile with a rear compartment having a soft folding top, initially for two passengers; later, with larger compartment and a couple of occasional seats, for four. The driver's (and footman's) seat was in front subject to the elements and, later, when a windscreen was provided, a soft roof could be fixed. Still later the chauffeur's compartment was endowed with low doors and eventually even side windows. The illustration shows an example of the very earliest coachbuilt designs, with the passenger compartment's window frames or pillars, including division, lowered into the doors and bodywork, making it effectively usable as a Touring Car. Cabriolet was originally a French term. An alternative French term is Décapotable. According to Henri-Labourdette, to be strict, Cabriolet implies ability to enclose an open vehicle, whereas Décapotable and Découvrable means facility to open an enclosed vehicle. In the 1920s, using the term Cabriolet alone usually implied a four or five seater automobile.

[1]Cabriolet ←

Important period

Ca. 1910 to 1930.

Variations

A later style Cabriolet had a passenger compartment with forward facing occasional seats for several passengers, and became known as Cabriolet de Ville/Convertible Town Car. Some coachbuilders did produce early and rare open two-seater owner-driver vehicles, sometimes with Rumble seat, anticipating the later two and three seater Cabriolet style automobiles—see below.

→ All-weather; Convertible Town Car; Convertible Stretch Limousine

[3]Cabriolet

The Cabriolet that emerged between the two World Wars, and particularly after the 1929 world slump, was the soft top American owner-driver Convertible and its European equivalent, i.e. a non-sporting two-door or four-

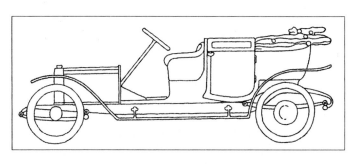

[2]Cabriolet. An early chauffeur-driven Cabriolet variation. The chauffeur had no weather protection.

door automobile usually based on the same wheelbase and seating arrangements as the normal production Coupe or Sedan. Normal seating capacity was two to five passengers, but long wheelbase Cabriolets would seat up to seven. Unlike the horse-drawn Cabriolet carriage and the Touring Car, the Cabriolet was intended to give its occupants the same weather protection as the enclosed Sedan, Limousine and Coupé bodyworks. Thus, it had well-engineered joints between the tight-fitting foldable top, doors and windshield as well as the framed glass side windows (which could be lowered out of sight). After World War II the number of Convertibles/Cabriolets based on the standard production Sedan (or Saloon/ Berline in Europe) has diminished, and particularly the modern European Cabriolet is often an up-market two-door two-seater, or even a full four-seater. It has usually a more or less pronounced Fastback rear body treatment. It is normally based on the manufacturer's standard components with the addition of luxury accoutrements and it is not uncommon for it to be equipped with a rollbar. The rear two seats in these automobiles are sometimes cramped, especially on vehicles constructed on a shorter wheelbase chassis. For illustration, *see Convertible Coupe.*

Origins and history

Nick Walker describes the evolution of the Cabriolet from the chauffeur-driven vehicle as "a drophead body with a division without even having enclosed drive. Soon, however, the requirement for the division was dropped, and it came to mean the same as an All-Weather; it began to replace that name during the mid-twenties ...." After World War II the styles of the Ameri-

can Convertible and the European Cabriolet diverged *(see further under Convertible)* and the European Cabriolets were seldom four-door four or five seaters. By the 1970s the number of traditional two to three seater Cabriolet cars had diminished considerably. The Cabriolet automobile became partly the prerogative of the specialist coachbuilder (some of which produce complete cars in small series based on chassis components delivered from the customer's production plant). This has led to the effect that in some cases the Cabriolet's traditional family likeness to the manufacturer's standard production Sedan style bodywork has been lost.

All-weather ←

Important period
Mid–1920s to the present.

Variations
A Faux-cabriolet is no Cabriolet but a Coupe automobile *(see ²Faux-cabriolet)*. In the 1920s Coupé Cabriolet was used to denote a two-door two to three seater Cabriolet, but today it has taken on a different meaning *(see ²Coupé-cabriolet)*. By Berline Cabriolet was meant four-door Convertible bodywork.

Language varieties
In North America Cabriolet has been periodically used by some manufacturers to denote their standard production Convertible Coupe body styles. In Britain the normal term for a two-door Convertible bodywork is Drop-head Coupé (DHC) or Drop-head Saloon, though Cabriolet is quite acceptable, and was favored especially by coachbuilders to denote four-door bodywork. In German the correct term is Kabriolett or Cabriolet (basically meaning a four-door vehicle) but Cabrio is a modern fairly vernacular variation. (Daim-

ler-Benz up to the mid–1950s designated their Cabriolet bodyworks on Mercedes-Benz chassis as Cabriolet A for a two-door two to three seater, Cabriolet B for a two-door four to five seater and Cabriolet D for a four-door vehicle seating five or more.) A German bodywork variant was the Cabrio-Limousine *(q.v.)*. In Italy Cabriolet is the normal term for a basically four-door vehicle, but Convertible or Vettura trasformabile are somewhat dated alternatives. Aperto ("open") is a very general Italian term used in today's parlance for all sorts of open or Convertible vehicles. It could also be contended that in Europe Cabriolet is being loosely used as a generic and very unspecific term for *any* type of car with a folding soft top.

American: Convertible Coupe or Convertible Sedan.

British: Drop-head Coupé or Cabriolet.

French: Cabriolet or Décapotable.

German: Kabriolett or Cabriolet.

Italian: Cabriolet or Convertible.

⁴Cabriolet

Grande Routière—a luxuriously appointed, coachbuilt two-door European car with ample space for luggage. Whereas the Gran Turismo is always closed, a Grande Routière can have open (Convertible) as well as closed (Coupe) bodywork.

→ *Grande Routière*

⁵Cabriolet

A limited production Supercar with a folding top.

→ *Supercar*

Cabriolet 2/3 Plätze

German for a two to three seater contemporary Convertible Coupe.

→ *Convertible Coupe*

Cabriolet à 2/3 places

French for a two to three seater Convertible Coupe.

→ *Convertible Coupe*

Cabriolet a 2/3 posti

Italian for a two to three seater Convertible Coupe.

→ *Convertible Coupe*

Cabriolet à 6-7 places

French for a long open Limousine with capacity for six to seven passengers.

→ *Pullman-Kabriolett*

Cabriolet a 6-7 posti

Italian for a long open Limousine with capacity for six to seven passengers.

→ *Pullman-Kabriolett*

Cabriolet a 7-9 posti

Italian for Convertible Stretch-limo.

→ *Convertible Stretch-limo*

Cabriolet Anglais

French way (obs.) of expressing a British two to three seater Convertible with Rumble seat.

→ *Rumble seat*

Cabriolet de Ville

A Coupé de Ville style automobile with a folding roof over the two-light rear passenger compartment aft of the glass division, making the vehicle completely open. The design also allows as a rule the front portion only of the folding roof to be rolled up (Walker). Seating capacity was five with occasional seats in the rear passenger compartment. The chauffeur's seat was normally open with the possibility to pull forward a canopy roof. The bodywork of this type of automobile was mostly coachbuilt.

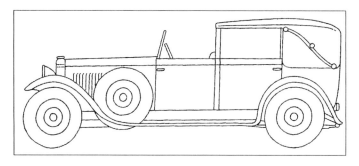

Cabriolet de Ville. This body style—originally French for Convertible Town Car—was the next evolutionary step from the early Cabriolet.

Origins and history

With prestige entering the issue, Cabriolet de Ville became the name for a fundamentally similar vehicle to the early chauffeur-driven Cabriolet automobile (²*Cabriolet*).

²*Cabriolet; Coupé de Ville* ←

Important period

1915 to 1930.

Variations

A 1920s coachbuilt variation was the small four-seater Cabriolet with a foldable top for the rear passengers only. It is not clear whether this small vehicle was in fact meant to be owner-driven.

Language varieties

In its day the Cabriolet de Ville body style was fairly rare compared to its enclosed opposite number, the Coupé de Ville. This may account for the dominance in Europe of the archetype French Cabriolet de Ville term.

American: Convertible Town-car, Town Cabriolet.

British: Cabriolet de Ville.

French: Cabriolet de Ville

German: Kupee-Kabriolett.

Italian: Cabriolet de Ville.

Cabriolet-Limousine

Full name of German Cabrio-Limousine.

→ *Cabrio-Limousine*

Cabriolet Stretch-limousine

British, and also used in some other Continental countries, for an open, extra long Limousine.

→ *Convertible Stretch-limo; Stretch-limo*

Cabriolet toit de 3 positions

French alternative name for Cabriolet-victoria.

→ *Cabriolet-victoria*

Cabriolet-victoria

A high-quality two-door car having front and rear seats and a Convertible top which can be placed in a semi-open position with the front part of the top folded and the rear part erect to resemble the old Victoria-top style, thus covering only the rear seats. The top can of course also be placed in a fully extended

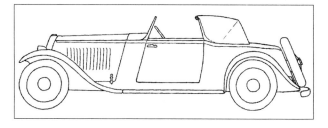

Cabrolet-victoria. A body style that carried many names during a fairly short period of popularity.

position as well as fully folded. Two side windows only. This bodywork style was sometimes in earlier times referred to as Milord or Coupé Milord.

2Calash; 3Milord; 3Victoria ←

Important period

1920s to 1940s.

Variations

A similar bodywork style but having the rear part of the top made of metal and fixed (i.e., not able to be folded down) is the Sedanca Coupé *(q.v.)*. The coachbuilt Cabriolet-victorias of the late 1930s became ever more luxurious.

Language varieties

American: Convertible Victoria.

British: Three-position Drop-head Coupé, Folding Head DHC.

French: Cabriolet-victoria, Cabriolet toit de 3 positions, Coupé Milord.

German: Kabriolett 3-Positionen Dach.

Italian: Cabriolet-victoria.

Cabrio-Limousine

Accepted and set abbreviation of Cabriolet-Limousine; German for a two- or four-door (Sedan) car with fully folding (including the rear window) soft sunshine type roof with fixed side window and door frames when the roof is folded back. A body style popular especially in Continental Europe during the periods before and after World War II. The British near equivalent, the Sunshine Saloon *(q.v.)*, had a partly or fully folding roof. This body style in two-door form is known in some countries as Cabrio-Coach.

Important period

Ca. 1930-1960.

Language varieties

American: Sunroof.

British: Sunshine Saloon.

French: Découvrable or Voiture Découvrable.

German: Cabrio- or Kabrio-Limousine.

Italian: Berlina a tetto apribile.

→ *Sunroof*

1Calash, Calash top

There are indications that the term Calash for a two-wheeled horse-drawn carriage (sometimes described as luxurious) was used in the United States (and also in England before the term Barouche was introduced) to denote a Calèche type of carriage with a Victoria-style folding top.

1Calèche ←

2Calash, Calash top

Calash top, in American parlance, used to denote a folding hood which could be positioned with the front part folded and the rear part erect, thus covering only the rear seats of a four or five seater car.

→ *Convertible Victoria*

1Calèche

In Continental Europe (and initially also in En-

Cabrio-Limousine. German term for the fully folding or roll-down Continental style of Sunroof.

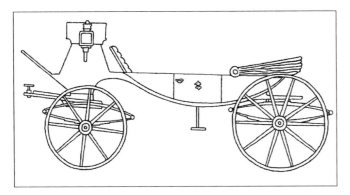

**¹Calèche. This illustration shows the later version of the Calèche/
Barouche, suspended on fully elliptic leaf springs.**

gland) an open four-wheeled horse-drawn carriage, built in various degrees of exquisiteness, with a passenger body initially suspended on C-springs, later on steel leaf springs, and two passenger seats facing each other and one forward folding hood. For the coachman and assistant in front there was a raised open seat with a back-rest.

Origins and history

The origin of the Calèche is variously described as Czech (Koleska), Polish (Kolaska) or Serbian (Kolica, diminutive of Kola = carriage). The term traces its ancestry to at least the 17th century. Originally it denoted a two-wheeled horse-drawn carriage. Although applied to a four-wheeled and quite differently styled carriage, some evidence indicates that the name reached France via Italy.

Important period

Second half of 17th through 19th centuries.

Variations

The folding top theme for the passengers was carried over to automobiles via the French four-wheeled Calèche carriage to the horse-drawn Landau *(q.v.)* and thenceforth into the Landaulet automobile bodywork style (al-

though the Landau carriage is heavier than the Calèche and has two folding tops). Victoria and Milord, near relations to the Calèche, have one seating bench only. (Interestingly, the Danish "kaleche" and Norwegian "kalesj" mean not only the whole carriage proper but also the folding top—*see* ²*Calash* above.)

Language varieties

After an initial period, the term Calèche in England, according to Sallmann, was in the 19th century superseded by Barouche *(q.v.)*. In Canada, however, Calèche was still current (*see* ³*Calèche*). The automobile derivation of this term, Landaulet, can be traced via Landau.

American: Barouche.
British: Barouche.
French: Calèche.
German: Kalesche.
Italian: Calèsse or Calèche.
→ ¹*Landau;* ¹*Calash*

²Calèche

A variation of the Calèche carriage, the Calèche à la Daumont, initiated by the French count d'Aumont around 1830, was an otherwise similar carriage but without a coachman and coachman's perch in front. Instead, one horse in each of the two or three pairs was saddled and controlled by a rider, the postillion. This way of gala transportation—without the coachman in front—became much favored with royalty, aristocracy and *corps diplomatiques* to give the public free sight of the passengers (and probably vice versa). Some Calèche carriages could be changed to the à la Daumont mode by removing the coachman and his perch.

³Calèche

A Canadian two-wheeled horse-drawn carriage with a folding top used for taking tourists around cities, such as Montreal and Quebec.

Calèsse

Italian for Calèche.
→ *Calèche*

California Top

Alternative name for All-year Top and Detachable.
→ *All-year Top*

¹Car

A light two-wheeled open horse-drawn carriage used in the late nineteenth and first decade of the twentieth century; e.g., the Governess Car/Cart (for illustration *see ¹Tonneau*) and the Ralli Car/Cart. There were Continental European variations to these designations; thus the rear-entrance Governess Car was known in France as Tonneau, and Rally was a variant but incorrect spelling of Ralli. Also, "Cart" was the

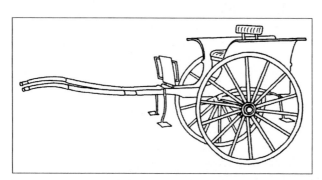

¹Car. Car is a term used for various vehicles—railroad cars, omnibuses and here, as Ralli Car, for a horse-drawn carriage.

norm on the Continent, rather than Car (Sallmann).
→ *¹Tonneau*

²Car

A railroad carriage of specified type for passengers (e.g. dining-car).

³Car

American for a railroad carriage.

⁴Car

French for omnibus (short for Auto-car).

⁵Car

The basket suspended beneath a balloon to contain the aeronaut(s), although normally referred to as a Gondola.

⁶Car

Car is nowadays the colloquial American and British term for any type of passenger vehicle for up to ca. 10 people without defining type of bodywork. Automobile is formally correct. Motor was an early British colloquial abbreviation for Motor car. Autocar and Motor car subsequently became just Car.

Language varieties
Formal American: Automobile.
Formal British: Motor car.
> *Formal French*: Automobile.
> *Colloquial French*: Voiture (Auto).
> *Formal German*: Pkw or PKW, short for Personenkraftwagen.
> *Colloquial German*: Auto, Wagen.
> *Formal Italian*: Autovettura, Automobile.
> *Colloquial Italian*: Macchina, Auto.

Cariole

Alternative spelling of Carriole.
→ *Carriole*

[1]Carriage

A horse-drawn vehicle for persons.
Origins and history
From Latin "carrus" via French "carier" to Middle English "cariage." Strictly speaking, "Carriage" meant originally a vehicle's frame undercarriage, or, in a modern idiom, the chassis of a vehicle.
Language varieties
American: Carriage.
British: Carriage.
French: Voiture hippomobile.
German: Kutsche.
Italian: Vettura, Carrozza.

[2]Carriage

A wheeled stand or support of a gun; a gun-carriage.

[3]Carriage

A British railroad car or coach for passengers.

Carrick

A light, open horse-drawn vehicle the bodywork back wall of which was characterized by an S or ogee shape.
Origins and history
According to various French sources Carrick is an English term. This is borne out by Robert Sallman's *Kutschenlexikon*, which states that the term originated in Ireland as a name for a cloak with many collars, entering the English language in 1805 and the German carriage terminology as Garrick in 1833. At the end of the 18th century Carrick denoted that the back wall had an ogee form. English carriage builders, however, did not use the term Carrick at all, preferring to describe the shape of the back wall as "ogee" or "briska" shaped.
Important period
19th century.
Variations
French carriage builders took over and applied the term to various carriage types, pronouncing them as Mylord-Carrick, Duc-Carrick or Phaéton-Carrick. Variations of these terms found subsequently their way into automobile bodywork terminology.
→ *Duc; Milord; Phaéton*

Carriole

A small hand-pushed or horse-drawn two-wheeled cart. This term exists in various permutations in different parts of the world, and has occasionally been used to describe an early Light car, or the bodywork of a car. In USA, Nash applied the model name Carriole in 1922–1924 to one of their low-priced Sedans. The term derives via the French *carriole* from Latin *carrus*. In contemporary colloquial French the word may have a derogatory meaning of a well used automobile.
Carrus ←

Carro funebre

Italian for Hearse.
→ *Hearse*

Carrosse

French for Gala or State Coach. (N.b. Not to be confused with Carrosserie, which means bodywork/coachwork.)
Carrozza ←

Carrosserie

French for bodywork.
→ *[2]Bodywork*

Carrosserie autoporteuse

French for unitary construction. An alternative term is Monocoque.
→ *Unitary construction*

Carrosserie deux volumes

French for Two-box or Fastback.
→ *Fastback*

Carrosserie monovolume

French for a bodywork without a front and rear Box, the nearest body style being that of the Minivan.
→ *[1]Minivan*

Carrosserie trois volumes

French for Three-box or Notchback.
→ *Notchback*

Carrozza

Italian for a heavy and luxurious horse-drawn ceremonial Coach manufactured and used in various forms and during a very long period of time for triumphal processions and state or gala occasions by heads of state, royalty, aristocracy, members of the *corps diplomatique* etc. By Carrozza is also meant a simpler four-wheeled carriage. (N.b. Not to be confused with Carrozzeria, which means bodywork/ coachwork.)

Origins and history

The origins can be traced to Latin *carruca*, a short description of which has been given by Pliny the Younger *(see Carruca)*. From its rather primitive beginnings the formal Roman Carrozza was developed into various and ever more comfortable permutations in many countries, until it was more or less replaced by the Berline in the 18th century.

Carruca ←

Important period

From the 16th to the 18th century.

Language varieties

English: Gala or State Coach.
French: Carrosse.
German: Prachtwagen, Hofkutsche, Karosse.
Italian: Carrozza.
→ *[1]Berline*

Carrozzeria

Italian for bodywork.
→ *[2]Bodywork*

Carrozzeria a due volumi

Italian for Two-box or Fastback.
→ *Fastback*

Carrozzeria a tre volumi

Italian for Three-box or Notchback.
→ *Notchback*

Carrozzeria autoportante

Italian for unitary construction (Monocoque).
→ *Unitary construction*

Carrozzeria monovolume

Italian for a bodywork without a front and rear Box, the nearest being Minivan.
→ *[1]Minivan*

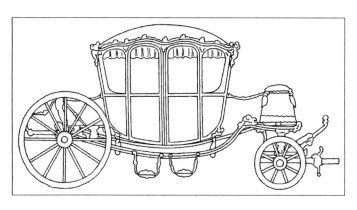

Carrozza. Italians were the earliest manufacturers and users of luxurious Gala and State Coaches.

Carruca

Carruca has been described by Pliny the Younger (Gajus Plinius Caecilius Secundus) in the 1st century as "a kind of four-wheeled wagon; travelling carriage, state coach." It was later used in Italian to denote an open Chariot and variously other horse-drawn carriage types. Early automobile terms, like Charabanc, can be traced via Char, Chariot etc.

→ *Carrozza; Chariot*
Carrus ←

Carruccio

Italian for Sedan Chair.
→ *²Sedan*

Carrus

Latin for a very early open, four wheeled, horse-drawn wagon. Various carriage and vehicle names stem from Carrus such as Carruca, Carriage, Carriole, Char, Charrette, Char à bancs (Charabanc), Chars de carneval, Char de combat, Chariot, Carretto, Karre. Variously and eventually these terms lead to Car.

→ *Car; Carruca*

Cart

Continental version of a horse-drawn Car.
→ *¹Car*

Char

French, from Latin *carrus*, an early two-wheeled open carriage or a four- or more wheeled carriage used for heavy loads or combat. Also contemporary English for an engine propelled armoured combat vehicle moving on tracks.

→ *Charabanc; Char funèbre*
Carrus ←

¹Charabanc

From the French Char à bancs, meaning a 19th century rustic, open horse-drawn carriage for transporting many people for a day in the country, sight-seeing, shooting etc. Two passenger benches were usually arranged crosswise but sometimes lengthwise behind the driver.

²Break ←

²Charabanc

An early open motor vehicle generally with two lengthwise rear benches for several passengers. Entry and exit to the passenger benches was through a rear central gate, usually of necessity because the chain rear-wheel drive front sprockets of the side drive-chains were located on both sides approximately at the ideal place for entrance to the rear seats through side doors. In Britain as late as the 1920s Charabancs were used as public service vehicles to carry eight or more passengers to one or more common destinations without stopping (like om-

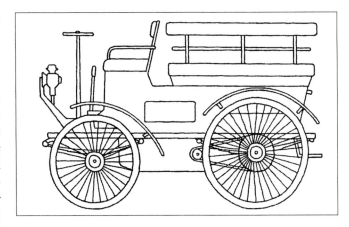

²Charabanc. The Charabanc was a comparatively heavy motor propelled vehicle for several passengers. Considerably lighter was the fairly similar Wagonette.

nibuses), picking up or setting down passengers along the route. In some countries in the 1920s large open vehicles for sightseeing were constructed on commercial vehicle chassis and had several rows of seats. These were also popularly called Charabancs.

Language varieties
American: Char-a-bancs, Charabanc.
British: Charabanc.
French: Char à bancs.
German: Charaban or Char à bancs.
Italian: Char à bancs.

Char à bancs

The original French term for Charabanc. An internationally known term with national spelling variations.
→ *Charabanc*

Char funèbre

French for Hearse.
→ *Hearse*

Chariot

From French Char, an ancient, usually two-wheeled, open horse-drawn carriage for battle, triumphal state processions, ceremonies and racing. The bodywork of this vehicle was of the simplest form, consisting merely of a curved shield of various forms in front of the driver, who had no seat but stood. In order to make the vehicle easy to maneuver, the body and the driver's standing point above the wheel axle were concentrated to one point of gravity. The term Chariot has been variously used for other kinds of early horse-drawn vehicles. Early automobile terms, like Charabanc, derive from Chariot.

The illustration shows a Roman Chariot for war and triumphal processions, to be drawn by several horses.
Char ←

Language varieties
American: Chariot.
British: Chariot.
French: Char Romain.
German: Streit- und Triumphwagen.
Italian: Biga.

Charrette

French term used in Italy for a light open or closed automobile in the first decade of the 20th century.
→ *[1]Voiturette*

Char Romain

French term for a two-wheeled war or racing Chariot.
→ *Chariot*

Chassis

English for the assembly of frame members, suspension, wheels and other components making up the framework that supports the body of a horse-drawn carriage or motor vehicle. Alternative term: Under-

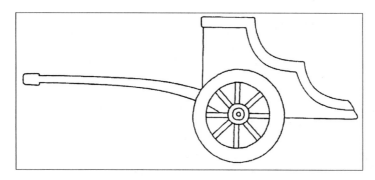

Chariot. The Roman Chariot was used both for war and triumphal processions.

carriage. *See also Platform and Unitary construction.*

Language varieties
American: Chassis.
British: Chassis.
French: Châssis.
German: Fahrgestell.
Italian: Autotelaio.

Châssis
French for Chassis.

Chauffeur-limousine
French for a large, completely enclosed chauffeur-driven automobile with the chauffeur separated from the large, luxurious passenger compartment, the "saloon," by a glass division which, in its most formal form, was permanently fixed. Normally occasional seats are provided for additional passengers. Four-door, normally six-windowed 7–9 seater. The rearmost side (Quarter) windows are usually quite large ones.

Important period
Mid–1920s to present (N.b. the use of the designation has lost out to plain Limousine).
→ *²Limousine*

Chummy
Informal and now obsolete term, it seems, used infrequently both in north America and Britain to describe the cramped interior of an Occasional four-seater body, best represented by certain pre-World War II cars; e.g., in America the Bantam, in Britain the small Austin and Morris cars.
→ *Close-coupled*

Citadine
French for a contemporary very small (city) car.
→ *Light car; Microcar*

Clarence
A large and heavy early 19th century British Coupé type of horse-drawn carriage named after the Duke of Clarence, who became King William IV. The original Clarence had bowed D-style front glass and capacity for four passengers. Later, this vehicle fitted out with luggage racks on the roof became popular in the Hackney trade for railroad station services, colloquially known as "Growlers."
→ *¹Brougham; ²Hackney*
¹Coupé ←

Close-coupled
British and American term for a four-windowed, usually four-door owner-driver automobile with a small passenger compartment and, therefore, short roof. *The Motoring Encyclopedia and Touring Gazetteer* (1934) describes Close-coupled as follows: "The close-coupled seating arrangement is a compromise between the two-seater and the full four-seater. It is really a development of the chummy body. The rear

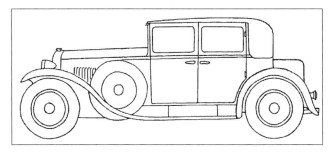

Close-coupled Sedan. The rear seat passengers in Sedans before World War II used to sit above the rear axle. Moving them forward resulted in a Close-coupled body style.

seats in a close-coupled body are arranged close up behind the front ones, often with the feet of the rear passengers accommodated under the front seats. Although extensive leg room is not to be expected in the rear seats in the smaller cars, the close-coupled seating enables two extra passengers to be carried with full weather protection, and at the same time permits good overall body lines to be secured."

Important period
1910 to present.

Variations
An American bodywork of this type, although strictly two-door, was usually termed Coach. Two- or four-door somewhat up-market variants are the Brougham and Club Sedan. A British Sports Saloon was lighter and faster, in addition to being Close-coupled. The nearest French equivalent to Close-coupled Saloon would be the Berline quatre places rapprochées or Coach.

Language varieties
Berlinette would also be an apposite but today seldom used French term for a smaller than standard (the "standard" size varying in different parts of the world) production Sedan. The same applies to the Italian Berlinetta. A German term that would be applicable here is Limousine, 4 Sitze.

American: Close-coupled Sedan.
British: Close-coupled Saloon.
French: Berline quatre places rapprochées, Berlinette.
German: Limousine, 4 Sitze.
Italian: Berlinetta.
→ *Club Sedan*

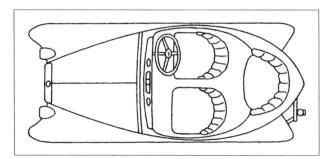

Cloverleaf. A central rear seat for a third passenger gave the body style the epithet Cloverleaf. There is no door for entrance to the rear seat.

Cloverleaf

Colloquial for an open or enclosed automobile having three-seater bodywork, the third (rear) seat being central.

Important period
1920–1930.

Language varieties
French: Trois places en trèfle.

Club Coupe

An American high-class four- to five-seater, two-door, four side-windowed Coupe style automobile built on the standard wheelbase Sedan chassis. A universal definition of this body style is lacking, but generally it appears that the passenger compartment size falls between the standard Coupe of the period under consideration and the normal Sedan body; i.e., the roof line is longer than the Coupe but shorter than the Sedan, and the lengthwise interior space is limited compared to the Sedan body style. This is the largest of the American Coupe body style variations.

Origins and history
The designation seems to derive from Club car, i.e. the railroad lounge or parlor car (Flammang & Kowalke), which would indicate that the Club Coupe embodies comfort and appointments not normally found in standard pro-

duction Coupes. This is also reflected in the unit price.

³Coupé ←

Important period
Mid–1920s to mid–1950s.

Variations
→ *Club Sedan*

Club Sedan

An American usually high-class five-passenger (occasionally six passenger), two- or four-door small-cabin Sedan manufactured on a standard Sedan chassis but having a shorter roof and somewhat limited lengthwise interior space compared to the normal Sedan from the period around World War II. Four side windows only and small panel Quarters. This is the smallest of the Sedan body style variations.

Origins and history

The designation seems to come from Club car, i.e. the lounge or Parlor car in a railroad train (Flammang & Kowalke), and as such it would appear that the Club Sedan was a nimbler and better appointed version of the normal Sedan during the period under consideration. This is reflected in the unit price. This body style, in a somewhat earlier period, was also known under the designation of Brougham. A comparable and also somewhat earlier body

style was the Coach *(see ²Coach)*. The variability of terms leads to the suspicion that auto manufacturers looked at catchy name combinations rather than strict body style definitions.

³, ⁴Sedan ←

Important period
Mid–1920s to mid–1950s.

Variations
→ *Club Coupe*

¹Coach

A large four-wheeled initially open, later enclosed horse-drawn carriage for several passengers, with two doors and an elevated seat in front for the coachman. Suspension could be either by leather straps or steel leaf springs. The illustration shows the leather strap short body design with the Dorsay back form.

Origins and history

This horse-drawn carriage style was invented circa 1460 in the Hungarian township of Kocs and was called Kocsi (short for Kocsi szekér). It was of light construction and the bodywork was initially fixed unsuspended on two wheel axles.

¹Kutsche ←

Important period
15th through 19th century.

Variations

The Hungarian carriage-builders became famous for their craftsmanship, and their carriages and carriage design spread via Austria over Europe and further to many parts of the world. It should be noted that car-

Club Sedan. The "Club" term imparted class to a small-cabin Sedan.

¹**Coach. This Coach is the short-bodied Anglo-American counterpart of the Berline-Coupé carriage.**

with smaller interior space and shorter roof than the Sedan, usually without a trunk.

Origins and history

It seems reasonable to assume that the two-door similarity between the horse-drawn carriage and the motor vehicle led

riages represented by the below language varieties in their respective countries do not correspond in all details to the above definition; on the contrary, technical development to the carriage body as well as to the undercarriage did take place over the years, some

²**Coach. An American two-door small-cabin car which preceded the somewhat larger and later two-door Sedan.**

of which will be evident in the accompanying illustration. Many detail variations existed between Coaches produced in different countries.

Language varieties

Coach is also the term still used in English for heavy formal carriages for state occasions and gala *(see Carrozza).*

American: Coach.
English: Coach.
French: Coche.
German: Kutsche.
Italian: Cocchio.
→ *¹Berline*

²Coach

American for an enclosed two-door automobile for four or five passengers

to the application of this carriage name to the car. The similar lack of facility to carry luggage may have been a contributing factor. The 1920s Coach automobile was the forerunner of the 1930s two-door Sedan. A comparable bodywork style is the Club Coupe *(q.v.).*

Important period
1923–1935.
→ *³Sedan*

³Coach

French and Italian (also German in German-speaking part of Switzerland) for an enclosed two-door, minimum four-seater car, usually two-light (two side windows) and as a rule having a shorter roof and more restricted interior space than the normal Berline (Sedan) type of car. Coach is also known to have been applied in France, generally before World War II, to two-door, four-light cars smaller than a Berline (in which case the term Berlinette would perhaps have been pertinent).

[4]Coach

American for a large passenger vehicle or a bus operating according to a schedule along a fixed route. British for a single-decker bus, usually a comfortable one for longer journeys.

[5]Coach

American for a railroad passenger car for day travel and for a trailerized home. British for a railway carriage.

[1]Coachwork

The design and process of manufacturing the external shell for a carriage or an automobile.

[2]Coachwork

The external shell of a carriage or an automobile (usually custom-built).
Language varieties
American: Coachwork, Bodywork.
British: Coachwork, Bodywork.
French: Carrosserie.
German: Karosserie.
Italian: Carrozzeria.
→ *Bodywork*

Cocchio

Italian for Coach.
→ *[1]Coach*

Coche

French for Coach.
→ *[1]Coach*

Coda Bateau

Italian bodywork designation to specify a pointed Boattail body style.
→ *Bateau*

Coda Bordino

Italian bodywork designation to specify a Bordino style tail.
→ *Bordino*

Colonnade, Colonnade Hardtop

Term applied by General Motors in the mid–1970s to two- and four-door heavily pillared Hardtop bodywork styles constructed to meet American federal rollover standards (Flammang & Kowalke).

Combi

Another spelling of Kombi, probably emanating from the Dutch Combinatiewagen.
→ *Kombi*

Commerciale

French model name for a bodywork style with seating and luggage capacity comparable to a Hatchback Sedan (Commerciale being a very early application of the Hatchback design by Citroën). In spite of the utilitarian sounding designation, this type of car had rarely any commercial vehicle connotations. (Familiale [*q.v.*] is in French the Station Wagon type of bodywork.)
→ *Hatchback Sedan*

Compact

Term used in combination to indicate smaller automobile bodywork size than normal. It should be observed, however, that "compact" with regard to cars carries different values between the United States and the rest of the world.

Thus, an American Compact could be considered in Europe a fairly large vehicle, whereas a European Compact could be seen as a Microcar in the USA.

American: Compact.
British: Compact.
French: Compacte.
German: Kompakt.
Italian: Compatto.

Compacte

French for Compact.
➙ *Compact*

Compact minivan

A small Minivan; in effect a mix between a large Minivan and a small Station Wagon. The bodywork is usually based on the Platform of a small Sedan, but is short and high. Seating capacity up to six.

Origins and history

The Renault Scénic Compact minivan evolved as a European version of the normal Minivan. Renault in the mid–1990s was the progenitor of this style of bodywork.

[2]*Minivan* ←

Language varieties

American: Compact minivan.
British: Mini People-carrier, MPC.
French: Monocorps, Monovolume.

Compact minivan. A modern small Minivan/Station Wagon style of automobile.

German (formal and technical): Mehrzweck-Fahrzeug.
German (general): MPW, Minivan.
Italian: Monovolume.

Compatto

Italian for Compact.
➙ *Compact*

Competition

A model name sometimes used informally to denote a car suitable for racing. Rarely an official type or model name designated by the vehicle maker. The same can be said generally to apply for the French and Italian counterparts—Compétition or Course and Competizione or Corsa, respectively, although Compétition was used by Delahaye for one model, and one German manufacturer has in recent decades given Corsa as model name for one of its small Sedans. *See also C.*

Compétition

French for Competition.
➙ *Competition*

Competition Cars

➙ *Racing*

Competizione

Italian for Competition.
➙ *Competition*

Conduite Intérieure

French basically for Enclosed or Inside drive. Originally the term indicated that the chauffeur was no longer sitting in the open (as in a Coupé—*see* [2]*Coupé)*, but had full weather protection (as in a Limousine—*see* [2]*Limousine)*, still with the glass division between him and the rear passenger compartment. A variation of meaning later took place. In accordance with the increasing numbers of enclosed owner-driven cars, around 1930, Conduite Intérieure, or just Conduite, came to be used as meaning *not* chauffeur-driven; i.e., effectively the same as Owner-driver. With this later connotation, in the period before World War II, the term would typically have been applied to Sedan bodied cars in French, but it was also, and somewhat surprisingly, used for various other kinds of enclosed bodywork. In fact, the "Intérieur" part was often dropped—a Coupé car could, rather unnecessarily, be termed "Conduite-coupé," and a Cabriolet "Conduite-cabriolet." In Italy and Germany Guida interna and Innenlenker mean Enclosed drive in the original sense only; i.e., that the chauffeur is fully weather protected in his compartment in front of the division.

Important period
1910s to 1950s.

Language varieties
American: Enclosed drive, Inside drive.
British: Inside drive, Enclosed drive.
French: Conduite Intérieure
German: Innenlenker, Innensteuer.
Italian: Guida interna.

Continental Coupé
A British Grand Tourer. A two-door fixed-head or drop-head car with amenities for two people to travel long distances in comfort and luxury. The Continental Coupé style was a low-production, high-cost car. An archetypal example of this vehicle is the Mulliner bodied Bentley Continental of 1954–55.
→ *Grand Tourer; Gran Turismo*

Convertibile
Italian, nowadays seldom used, alternative term for Cabriolet.
→ [1, 2, 3]*Cabriolet*

Convertible
A Convertible is a non-sporty two-door or four-door automobile with a foldable tight-fitting top and proper glass side windows that can be lowered out of sight. The Convertible is often based on the same wheelbase and seating arrangements as the manufacturer's normal enclosed production Coupe or Sedan. It seats from two to seven passengers. The term Convertible can also imply a removable top—see [2]*Hardtop*.
All-weather ←

Important period
Late 1920s to present. In the period 1977–1981 no American Convertibles were produced.

Variations
Convertible can be specified as Convertible Coupe (previously two or three seater, later five or six seater) or Convertible Sedan (four-door bodywork). In the USA in the 1930s some cars that were in effect Convertible Coupes were termed, misleadingly, Roadsters.

Language varieties
The original and normal international term for Convertible is Cabriolet. Drop-head Coupé (DHC) or Drop-head Saloon are British alternatives to Cabriolet. Whereas Cabriolet always means a foldable soft roof or top, Convertible could infer both a soft top and a removable hard top. The originally French term Cabriolet has been used during various periods by some American auto manufacturers to describe their standard production Convertible Coupe body styles. Soft-top or Rag-top are American colloquial varieties of Convertible.

American: Convertible.
British: Drop-head Coupé (DHC) or Drop-head Saloon.
French: Cabriolet or Décapotable.
German: Kabriolett or Cabriolet.
Italian: Cabriolet or Convertible.
➝ *³Cabriolet; Convertible Coupe; Convertible Sedan*

Convertible Coupe

American for a two-door collapsible top, non-sporty automobile, earlier with two to three seater (on a wide bench seat) bodywork, but since the 1950s very seldom with space for fewer than four passengers. Cabriolet was the French progenitor of the Convertible body style.

Language varieties
American: Convertible Coupe.
British: Drop-head Coupé (DHC).
French: Cabriolet à 2/3 places.
German: Cabriolet 2/3 Plätze, Kupee-Kabriolett (arch.).
Italian: Cabriolet a 2/3 posti.
➝ *³Cabriolet*

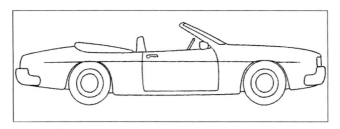

Convertible Coupe. An American Cabriolet-style bodywork.

Convertible Limo

American for a long open Limousine with seating for six to seven passengers. For illustration *see Pullman-Kabriolett*.

Language varieties
American: Convertible Limo.
British: 4-door Drop-head Limousine.
French: Cabriolet/Décapotable à 6-7 places.
German: Pullman-Kabriolett, Pullman-Cabriolet.
Italian: Cabriolet a 6-7 posti.
➝ *Pullman-Kabriolett*

Convertible Sedan

American four-door, five to seven seater Cabriolet. One or two American manufacturers produced this body style as late as mid–1960s. Today, production of Convertible Sedans is all but extinct.

All-weather ⬅

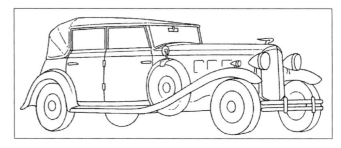

Convertible Sedan. A large four-door soft top automobile.

Language varieties
In some languages Cabriolet, like Sedan, has the fundamental significance of a four-door vehicle.
American: Convertible Sedan.
British: Drop-head Saloon, Cabriolet.
French: Berline Cabriolet.
German: Kabriolett or Cabriolet.
Italian: Cabriolet or Convertibile.
➝ *³Cabriolet*

Convertible Stretch-limo

An American stretched open, always chauffeur-driven, Limousine, usually for state occasions. After the assassination of president John F. Kennedy in a Convertible Stretch-limo in 1963 this bodywork has lost some of its popularity.

Language varieties
American: Convertible Stretch-limo.
British: Drop-head Stretch-limousine.
French: Voiture Décapotable à 7-9 places, Stretch-limo Décapotable.
German: Pullman-Kabriolett, Pullman-Cabriolet.
Italian: Cabriolet Stretch-limo, Cabriolet a 7-9 posti.
→ *Stretch Limo*

Convertible Town-car

A Town-car with a glass division (which is usually possible to lower out of sight) and a completely foldable rear top over the whole passenger compartment aft of the division. The design allows also the front portion only of the folding roof to be rolled up (Walker). The bodywork of these automobiles was usually custom built. For illustration *see Cabriolet de Ville.*

Coupe de Ville ←
Language varieties
American: Convertible Town-car, Town Cabriolet.
British: Cabriolet de Ville.
French: Cabriolet de Ville
German: Kupee-Kabriolett.
Italian: Cabriolet de Ville.
→ *Town-Car*

Convertible Victoria

American for Cabriolet-victoria. A two-door car with a soft top which could be placed in a semi-open position, with the front part of the top folded and the rear part erect, Victoria style, thus covering only the rear seats. Typical for this bodywork style were the two side windows only; there were no rear Quarter lights. For illustration—*see Cabriolet-victoria.*

Important period
Mid–1920s to 1940.
Variations
In the past in the United States the Convertible Victoria name was also applied by coachbuilding companies to automobile models that did not have the semi-open top feature, not infrequently including regular Convertible Coupes.
Language varieties
Calash top was an alternative but now obsolete American name for this semi-open top style.
→ *Cabriolet-victoria;* [2]*Calash 2*

Corbillard

French for Hearse.
→ *Hearse*

Corsa

Italian for Competition when applied as a type name.
→ *Competition*

Corps

French for Box.
→ *Box*

Coupe

American for Coupé.
→ *Coupé*

Coupé

The originally French term Coupé has undergone many significant bodywork style changes during a long time. The first period comprises the horse-drawn Coupé up to the beginning of the 20th century (as per [1]*Coupé*, below), the second was the period when the five to six seater Berline automobile (Sedan) was halved to form the true two to three seater Coupé (as per [2, 3, 5]*Coupé* below) and the third period is the contemporary one, where the Coupé car bodywork has grown to hold up to five persons (as per [4]*Coupé* below) without constituting either a two-door Sedan or any of its European correlatives. In many countries and languages the term Coupé has come to be applied to various forms of small enclosed rooms or compartments for people in all sorts of wheeled vehicles, and to numerous car bodywork permutations, all with a fixed, solid top (roof) without evidence of having been cut off, as the name suggests (Fr. "coupé"), from anything.

[1]Coupé

A single- or twin-horse-drawn enclosed, elegant four-wheeled carriage, originally for two passengers, having a windowed door on each side and a front glass window, with an outside seat for the coachman in front of the passenger compartment. Suspension could be either by leather belts or elliptic steel leaf springs. The illustration shows the steel spring design with the stepped back form.

Origins and history

By cutting off (from French verb "couper") the front part of a Berline carriage the requirement for a smaller passenger compartment was met. In practical terms, therefore, this vehicle is a short version of a Berline carriage. Coupé carriages mostly used in town traffic had lanterns placed high on the body, whereas carriages for country use had their lanterns low mounted in order to light up the road in front as much as possible. Early models would sometimes have a rear "sword case" to carry weapons etc. The rounded back of the original 18th century Coupé was called, for some unaccountable reason, Dorsay (see illustration of *horse-drawn Coach*). The Dorsay back was generally replaced in the 19th century for a stepped back body style in order to accommodate elliptic steel springs (see [1]*Coupe* illustrated here).

[1]*Berline* ←

Important period

18th and 19th century.

Variations

A Coupé body on a horse-drawn undercarriage should have, strictly speaking, seating for just two passengers (Coupé Simple), but with a small backward facing front bench seat within the compartment four passengers could be carried. The British equivalents of Coupé were the lighter, single horse Brougham carriage, commissioned by Lord Brougham in the 1830s, and the larger, Three-quarter Clarence, which became also

[1]**Coupe. When the Berline body was shortened the Berline Coupé, or just Coupé, resulted.**

used as a vehicle for public hire. The Coupé carriage eventually became widely used and very popular; it also was much used by medical doctors as the Doctor's Coupé. The Coupé carriage was the precursor of the Coupé, and later Coupé de Ville, automobile.

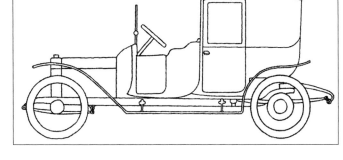

²Coupé. The early Coupé automobile's passenger compartment followed in general conception the horse-drawn Coupé.

Language varieties

According to Robert Sallmann the very first Coupé carriages, around the end of the 17th century, were called Berlingot in France, probably derived from Berline. Later the French term became Berline coupée, then Berline Coupé and finally abbreviated to just Coupé. The Coupé is an almost internationally established term, although in Britain the normal types of horse-drawn carriage, constructed for the same purposes as the Coupé, were the Brougham and Clarence carriages mentioned above. The Coupé name, although well-known in Germany, had two German language varieties, Kupee and Halbberline, the latter meaning literally "half-Berline."

→ *¹Brougham; Clarence; Halbberline*

²Coupé

An early Coupé automobile having originally a small two-door enclosed, elegant compartment for two passengers. The chauffeur's seat was in the open in front of the passenger compartment. In later versions the chauffeur became somewhat better protected by means of a windshield. The bodyworks of the earliest specimens were without exception coachbuilt.

Origins and history

The first Coupé car bodywork originated from its horse-drawn counterpart. The courageous people who believed in the automobile wanted, unsurprisingly, their first motor propelled Coupé to resemble their horse-drawn carriage that it replaced, which explains the external appearance of the first Coupé cars.

¹Coupé ←

Important period

First two decades of the 20th century.

Variations

A version with a more luxuriously appointed enclosed compartment and the facility for the chauffeur to be protected by a pull-out roof was also produced. This vehicle became eventually known as the Coupé de Ville or (in the United States) Brougham and Town Car or (in Britain) Brougham.

→ *²Brougham; Coupé de Ville*

³Coupé

A true Coupe car has a very small two-door enclosed fixed-head short top closed compartment for just the driver and one passenger, sometimes with a Rumble seat. Later, larger Coupe bodies seating three and four passengers were built. The three-window Coupe

³**Coupé. An early 1920s owner-driver Coupe automobile.**

has only two side windows, whereas the five-window variation has four. The rear part of the bodywork was traditionally of the Notchback *(q.v.)* style.

Origins and history

In the twenties the genuine small cabin Coupe concept became diluted, and this bodywork style developed in the United States, parallel with the original small variation, into a larger Coupe car seating sometimes as many as four and after World War II even six, thereby approaching the full two-door Sedan body style. The Coupe bodywork, especially in the United States, was usually based on the standard production Sedan, and in Europe on the Saloon/Berline bodywork, both embodying the Sedan's's/Saloon's chassis components, wheelbase and bodywork length. This resulted in a mid-chassis

³**Coupé. The 1930s Coupe was based on the standard series production Sedan chassis.**

location of the driver and the front seats, identical with that of the Sedan/Saloon. The Coupé car bodywork style was therefore in effect a result of cutting off the *rear* part of the Sedan top—in contrast to the horse-drawn Coupé, as per *¹Coupé* above, which had had the *front* part cut off its Berline body.

²Coupé ←

Important period

From the mid–1910s to World War II.

Variations

American Coupes came in various permutations, from the simple two-seater Business Coupe (externally sometimes recognizable through the lack of front Quarter ventilation windows in the doors) through the "normal" one and the Club Coupe, these two eventually providing space for several passengers. Extra seating could also be provided by a Rumble seat. "Double Date Coupe" was a delightful name given by Studebaker in 1941 to one of their five passenger Coupe models. A couple of odd four passenger Coupe versions having doors that opened either at the front or at the rear were coachbuilt around 1930 by Brunn in USA and Weymann in England—the front door hinges must have functioned as locking devices when opened by the front door handle, and vice versa. Not surprisingly, the American Coupe during the later part of the important period was substantially larger than its European counterpart. In England in the 1920s, a Coupé having a rather spacious four-light but still only two-seater compartment could—somewhat astonishingly—be termed Coupé Limousine (according to Shepherd, "a rather rare type of body"), the Limousine part of the name going back to "shelter/enclosure" *(see ¹Limousine)*. It must have been a mistake when LaFayette, according to 1923 factory records, applied Coupe to a *four*-door *six*-windowed vehicle. A Hardtop Coupe is a Coupé car with a fixed metal roof imitating the canvas top of a Convertible. A large, fast and comfortable, usually coachbuilt, two-door Coupé style car, essentially a two-seater with two occasional rear seats or four-seater, would best be described as a Gran Turismo *(q.v.)*.

Language varieties
American: Coupe.
British: Coupé or Fixed-head Coupé.
French: Coupé.
German: Coupé or Kupee.
Italian: Coupé.
→ *Club Coupe;* [2,3]*Faux-Cabriolet;* [1]*Hardtop*

⁴Coupé

An enclosed modern two-door fixed-top up-market Coupe. The American variation is large, seats up to six persons and has more or less taken over the role of the pre–World War II traditional two-door Sedan. Its normal contemporary European counterpart is an up-market two-door two-seater with almost always two comfortable rear seats or sometimes even a full five-seater having somewhat less comfortable rear seating. Always four side windows. This Coupe style has either the traditional Notchback or a more or less pro-nounced Fastback rear body treatment. It is normally based on the manufacturer's standard chassis components with the addition of luxury accoutrements. The rear seats in vehicles constructed on shorter wheelbase chassis may be cramped.

Origins and history
After World War II the traditional small cabin two to three seater American Coupe had gone out of production. Two decades later, and by the 1970s also in Europe, the number of traditional two to three seater Coupé cars had diminished considerably. The production of such cars had become partly the prerogative of the specialist coachbuilder (some of which produced complete cars with special bodies in small series based on more or less standard production components delivered from the maker) and had in some instances lost their previous characteristic exterior likeness to their standard production Sedan brethren.

³Coupé ←

Important period
Post World War II to date.

Variations
After World War II the Coupé car in its original strictly two to three seater permutation for just the driver and one or two passengers had all but disappeared. The ensuing American Coupe offers normally ample space for five or six passengers, whereas in the European and Far East variation rear-seat passengers have generally rather more limited space. In the decades before and after World War II some Coupé cars on both sides of the Atlantic were manufactured with a fixed metal roof imitating the canvas hood of a Convertible. This is the Hardtop or Faux-cabriolet body-work style. Another variation is a modern automobile having two doors and a

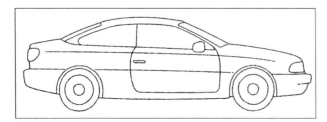

[4]Coupé. The modern Coupe bodywork has grown to be able to take—in extreme cases—up to six persons.

rear hatch door which includes the rear window—*see Hatchback Coupe*. A modern two-door Coupé with a rigid metal roof that can be folded and stowed into the luggage compartment can be found described under Coupé Cabriolet *(q.v.)*.

→ [2, 3]*Faux-cabriolet;* [1]*Hardtop*

Language varieties

With the term Coupé applied to this modern, rather large bodywork style it has acquired a wider interpretation. In fact, according to Flammang & Kowalke, some cars carry the Sedan designation on factory documents. There exist other, and perhaps more fitting, terms that could be applied to this contemporary Coupe bodywork style in order to differentiate it from the true two to three seater Coupe; in American English the well-established "Coach" or "two-door Close-coupled Sedan," in British English "two-door Close-coupled Saloon," in French "Berlinette," in German "Coupé 4 Sitze" and in Italian "Berlinetta."

[5]Coupé

A fixed-head version of a two-door, strictly two-seater high-performance Sports Car is often denoted Coupé or Sports Car, but should preferably be specified as a Sports Coupé. The distinctive bodywork difference between a front-engined traditional non-sporting Coupé and a front-engined, rear-wheel driven Sports Coupé is obvious from the driver's position: In the two-seater Sports Coupé, except for a mid-engined one, the driver and passenger sit back close to the rear axle, whereas in a normal (non-sporting) Coupe the driver and passenger sit much farther forward in the car. For illustration *see Sports Coupé*.

→ *Sports Coupé*

[1]Coupé Cabriolet, Coupé-cabriolet

Coupé Cabriolet was a little used and now obsolete British and French term for an enclosed two- or four-seater car with a two-door soft top convertible bodywork; for all intents and purposes a Convertible Coupe.

Origins and history

This term originated when the Coupé bodywork was first designed as a soft top variation. Otherwise, the origins and history of this bodywork are the same as those detailed under [3]*Cabriolet*.

Coupé ←

Important period

The term Coupé Cabriolet was used mainly in approximately the decades prior to and after World War I before the abbreviation to just Cabriolet took over completely in the late 1920s.

Language varieties

No language varieties to this designation have been found. It can therefore be considered an international term. It should be noted, however, that the German designation Kupee-Kabriolett refers to both (arch.) Convertible Coupe and the Cabriolet de Ville body style *(q.v.)*.

→ [3]*Cabriolet*

²Coupé Cabriolet, Coupé-cabriolet

Coupé-cabriolet is a contemporary international term for a two- or four-seater open two-door car with a hard metal roof which, with power assistance, can be folded and stowed into the baggage compartment, thereby making it in effect a Convertible car. With the roof closed the vehicle gives a visual impression of being a fully enclosed Coupe. Fairly recently adopted American and German terms for this style are ²Hardtop Convertible and Stahlfaltdach-Cabrio.

Origins and history

The first car designed with a collapsible hard metal roof that could be stowed in the car's trunk appears to have been a Peugeot in 1933. In 1935 and 1937 Peugeot again presented automobiles having a similar collapsible hard roof arrangement. Both were sub-type designated Eclipse. With a comparable roof design American Ford produced the Skyliner Retractable in the 1950s and Daimler-Benz introduced their Mercedes-Benz type SLK in the 1990s. In the year 2000 Peugeot again presented their collapsible roof style, this time an electric folding Hardtop in the type 206, sub-type designated CC for Coupé-cabriolet. A number of other manufacturers have followed suit.

→ ⁴Coupé
Cabriolet ←

Important period

1930s to present, with many and long intervals.

Language varieties

American: ²Hardtop Convertible.
German: Stahlfaltdach-Cabrio.

Coupé Chauffeur

French variant term for a Coupé de Ville automobile with a small passenger compartment. The bodywork of this type of automobile was mostly coachbuilt.

→ Coupé de Ville

Coupé de Ville

A chauffeur-driven automobile with coachbuilt enclosed luxurious rear passenger compartment for two or three passengers, usually with foldable occasional seats facing backwards. There were side windows in the two doors only. The chauffeur's seat was in the open but he could pull out and fix a soft canopy roof to the windshield for weather protection. It was unusual for a Coupé de Ville vehicle to have facilities for carrying luggage, for, after all, "de Ville" implies "for town [use]."

Origins and history

With prestige entering the issue, Coupé de Ville appears to have become the accepted name for a basically similar vehicle to the earlier chauffeur-driven Coupé automobile.

²Coupé ←

Important period

1915 to 1935.

Variations

The Brougham is a Coupé de Ville with special bodywork design features, particularly favored by British coachbuilding enterprises (see ²Brougham). Larger Coupé de Ville cars were characterized by having a more spacious passenger compartment and two Quarter side windows in addition to the door windows each side—these were usually termed Coupé Limousine. An automobile with Coupé de Ville-type of bodywork with a completely folding roof over the passenger compartment aft of the glass division was the Cabriolet de Ville. A car with Coupé de Ville type of bodywork but with a folding roof over

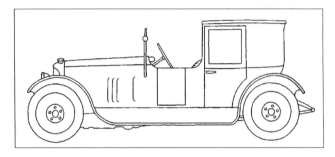

Coupé de Ville. Developed from the first motorized Coupe (²Coupé) was the more expensive Coupé de Ville.

the rear Quarter only is a Landaulet. Subsequently, when the chauffeur was allowed a fixed roof and the complete comfort of enclosure, the body style, still with a glass division, became a Limousine. The American Cadillac company for many years, not very appropriately, applied "Coupe de Ville" to one of their more expensive—but body stylewise quite normal—Coupe models.

Language varieties

The shorter, original, variation of the Coupé de Ville body was sometimes called Coupé Chauffeur, particularly in French speaking countries. The term Coupé de Ville was internationally used, but there were also specific national variations, such as the following:

American: Town Car, Brougham.

British: Coupé de Ville, Brougham.

French: Coupé de Ville, Coupé Chauffeur.

German: Stadtcoupé, Coupé de Ville.

Italian: Coupé di città, Coupé de Ville.

Coupé di città

Italian alternative name for Coupé de Ville.

Coupé de Ville ←

Coupé di città, 4 vetri

Italian alternative name for Coupé Limousine.

Coupé Limousine ←

Coupé Docteur

French for Doctor's Coupé.

→ *Doctor's Coupé*

Coupé d'Orsay

Designation given sometimes to a coachbuilt luxurious Coupé automobile. For an explanation of the origins of the name— see *d'Orsay, Dorsay.*

Coupé-Landau

German for Coupé Landaulet.

→ *Coupé Landaulet*

Coupé Landaulet

In practical terms an owner-driver small Landaulet automobile for two or three persons. Herbert Butler in *Motor Bodywork* (1924) describes a "Coupé-lette" (*sic*) as having a wide Brougham door and the roof fixed as far as the hind standing pillar. The head can be taken partly down and the trunk has a Rumble seat, resulting in a seating capacity of four passengers.

Origins and history

A requirement for a small Landaulet led to this bodywork style, which, however, enjoyed a limited time of popularity in England and USA.

Landaulet ←

Important period

1915–1925.

Variations

Although mainly American and British, a few vehicles of this bodywork style are known to have been built also in Germany, and there termed Coupé-Landau. In the 1980s a German specialist in Convertible conversions produced a Coupe top for open cars having a rear Quarter that could be opened

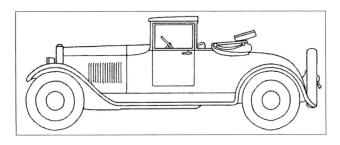

Coupé Landaulet. A small two or three seater embodying the collapsible rear Landaulet-style roof.

Landaulet-style and also transformed into a Targa style vehicle by openable roof panels *(see Targa/Targa top)*.

Language varieties
American: Coupelet.
British: Coupélet.
French: Coupé Landaulet.
German: Coupé-Landau.
Italian: Coupé Landaulet.

Coupelet
American and British for Coupé Landaulet.
→ *Coupé Landaulet*

[1]Coupé Limousine
A rare British fixed-head Coupé auto body style in the 1920s. [3]*Coupé*.

[2]Coupé Limousine
Coupé Limousine in French referred to a large Coupé de Ville automobile with an enclosed luxurious rear compartment for five to seven passengers, two or three of them on foldable extra seats, usually facing forward. The passenger compartment was characterized by normally having two rear Quarter side windows in addition to the door windows each side. Always chauffeur driven. The chauffeur's seat was in the open, later with the possibility to pull forward or to fix a detachable canopy roof. The bodywork of this type of automobile was mostly coachbuilt.

Origins and history
Coupé de Ville ←
The Coupé Limousine was built on a longer wheelbase chassis to accommodate the larger passenger compartment (the original meaning of "coupé" having become distorted *–see Coupé*). When the chauffeur was allowed a fixed roof and later the comfort of complete enclosure, the vehicle, still with a glass division, became a Limousine.

Important period
1915-1935.

Variations
Not all Coupé Limousines had four side windows; a body style giving the rearmost passengers some measure of seclusion had paneled rear Quarters *(see Single)*.

Language varieties
In Continental Europe a car with this bodywork was often colloquially referred to merely as a Coupé or Coupé de Ville irrespective of passenger compartment size.

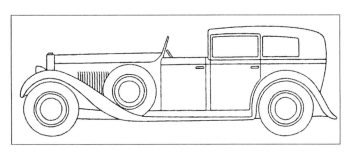

[2]Coupé Limousine. An automobile having a large capacity for passengers in the rear passenger compartment, the front ones facing forward on occasional seats.

American: Limousine Town Car, Limousine Brougham.

British: Sedanca, Limousine de Ville.

French: Coupé Limousine.

German: Coupé-Limousine, Stadt-Limousine, 4-fenstrig.

Italian: Coupé di Citta, 4 vetri or Coupé Limousine.

→ *Limousine Town Car*

Coupé Milord

Coupé Milord used to be French for a two-door Cabriolet automobile with a semi-foldable top; also termed just Milord (³*Milord*).

→ *Cabriolet-victoria*

Coupé Opéra

A term, possibly originating in the United States, for a luxurious Coupé car, the bodywork of which had a style derived from elegant horse-drawn carriages. The name was in some cases applied to denote the facility within the bodywork to carry an extra passenger or passengers, by e.g. occasional collapsible seating, or to allow smooth passage to the rear seats.

Coupé Simple

Variant name for a small horse-drawn Coupé for two passengers.

→ *¹Coupé*

Course

French for competition, straight line movement, quick march etc. Where applied to cars it usually represents a type name, although the initial C for competition is more common.

→ *Competition*

Couvre-tonneau

French for Tonneau-cover.

→ *⁴Tonneau*

¹Custom

An originally American bodywork term for a car that has been customized by adding fitments or modifying its bodywork to give the vehicle a personal appearance and character.

²Custom

Model name applied by (American) auto manufacturers.

Cyclecar

American and British for a very light and generally primitive open car having a single or two seats, the latter arranged in tandem, side-by-side or staggered. The bodywork was simple in the extreme, usually without doors, windshield and foldable top. For propulsion a single- or two-cylinder air-cooled engine that drove one or two rear wheels via friction discs, belts or chains. The American Cyclecar was limited to an engine size of 71 cubic inches (1.14 liters), whereas there were two British categories, one limited to an unladen weight of not more than 5.9 cwt (about 660 lbs or 300 kgs), the other to 7.5 cwt (about 840 lbs or 381 kgs). The Cy-

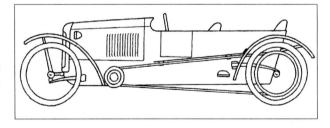

Cyclecar. A two-seater very light automobile, the illustration showing a tandem seating arrangement and belt-drive to the rear wheels.

clecar was in practical terms a four-wheeled motorcycle side car outfit, which it was intended to usurp.

Origins and history

The French tandem-seater Bédélia of 1910 seems to have given the impetus to the British and American Cyclecar production. The American Cyclecar was contemporary with the High-Wheeler and the Runabout but was in actual practice overtaken by the model T Ford. In Europe the Cyclecar lost popularity—except the sporting open Spider *(see ²Spider)*—when the proper, mass-produced Light Car appeared after World War I.

Important period

1910–1920, but some continued to be produced into the 1930s.

Variations

The number of Cyclecar variations during its short period of currency was large. Some were Three-wheelers. A very small number of enclosed Cyclecars were built, most of them in the Coupe body style. The French term Voiturette covers both Cyclecars and Light Cars.

→ *¹Voiturette*

-D-

d, D

Widely used contemporary subtype designation for either "diesel" or "direct" (injection).

Décapotable

French for folding or collapsible. According to Henri-Labourdette, to be strict, Décapotable implies ability to open an enclosed vehicle, whereas Cabriolet means possibility to enclose an open vehicle. The tautological combination Cabriolet Décapotable is not unknown in France.

→ *Cabriolet*

Décapotable à 6-7 places

French for a long convertible Limo with capacity for six or seven passengers.

→ *Pullman-Kabriolett*

Découvrable

French for Sunshine Saloon.

→ *Sunshine Saloon*

Deluxe, De Luxe

Some car manufacturers used to designate some of their products in the period ca. 1938–1970 Deluxe, De Luxe or DL for not very luxurious cars.

Demi-berline

French term around World War I for a small Berline automobile. The bodywork of a Demi-berline car was smaller than a Berline but larger than a strictly two-seater Coupé. French terms emerged later for subsequent vehicles with bodywork for the same purpose. These were the Coach and Berlinette *(q.v.)*.

→ *³Coach*

²Berline ←

Demi-tonneau

French for an open, light Tonneau automobile, in effect a Voiturette *(q.v.)*, with a separate rear space with rounded corners for two passengers only. Early chain-driven specimens had access for passengers to the rear seat through a door placed transversely in the middle of the rear bodywork wall. Later, around 1910, Demi-tonneaus could be seen sporting side-doors for entry to the rear seats following the introduction of propeller shaft drive. For further details, *see Tonneau*.

→ *²Tonneau*

Depot Hack

Early colloquial name in the USA for a Depot Wagon used as a taxi.

→ *Hackney*
Depot Wagon ←

Depot Wagon

Initial name for an early American motorized country wagon having three rows of two-person seats and wooden bodywork constructed of overlaid narrow wooden strips laid out in rectangular patterns. The rearmost seat was somewhat wider than the front and middle one, and could easily be taken out to provide space for luggage or goods. These vehicles were used for taking people to and from the railway station, carrying goods to the train depot, to commute to the city for work etc.

Origins and history

The Depot Wagon derived from the early pre–World War I Station Wagon. It found use also as a vehicle for hire, i.e. an early taxi, and was as such referred to as Depot Hack, the "Hack" part of the name probably emanating from Hackney *(q.v.)*.

Station Wagon ←
Important period
1920s to 1930s.
Language varieties
Depot Hack was a name really only

known in the USA. On the other hand the post–World War II sobriquet Woodie (not loved by everyone in America) for a wooden Station Wagon body became well-known worldwide.

→ *Woodie*

Detachable

Alternative term for All-year Top. Mainly in the 1920s, some auto manufacturers and coachbuilders both in America and Europe offered detachable "Winter" or "All-year" tops for one or several of their car models to make them habitable in all kinds of weather. These tops were complete windowed greenhouses from the beltline up, with arrangements for connecting to the main body, thereby transforming the open car effectively into an enclosed one. For illustration *see All-year Top*.

→ *All-year Top*

de Ville

French for "for town" (use). The chauffeur's compartment of "-de Ville" automobiles, e.g. Coupé de Ville, was originally devoid of weather protection but gradually gained a tall windshield and canopy roof. Subsequently, with a fixed roof the vehicle became a Limousine.

Variations

The "de Ville" suffix has been applied by Cadillac for many years to one of their two-door hardtop Coupe models without it having any relevance to the original Coupe de Ville bodywork style.

→ *Coupé de Ville*

DHC

Abbreviation for Drop-head Coupé. British for two-door Cabriolet.

→ *Convertible*

Dickey, Dickey seat
British for Rumble seat.
→ *Rumble seat*

DL
Abbreviation of Deluxe, used by some car manufacturers as a subtype designation.
→ *Deluxe*

Doctor's Coupé
The horse-drawn Coupé carriage *(see ¹Coupé)* became very popular with medical doctors as the Doctor's Coupé. The name was carried over to the early Coupé automobile, which was an enclosed car having a small two-seater body suitable for country doctors. Significant for an American car with this bodywork, which is similar to the Business Coupe, is the lack of a Rumble seat.

American: Doctor's Coupe.
British: Doctor's Coupé.
French: Coupé Docteur.
German: Doktor Coupé or Doktorwagen.
Italian: Coupé Docteur.
→ *Business Coupe; ³Coupé*

¹Dog Cart
Originally a two-wheeled open carriage for hunting and country use, driven by a single horse or a pair, the body providing space for hunting dogs under the rear seat(s), hence the name. Later, a four-wheeled version was developed which became very useful and popular.

²Dog Cart
Some late 19th century motor vehicles were produced very much on the lines of

¹Dog Cart. The Dog Cart had under-seat space for hunting dogs.

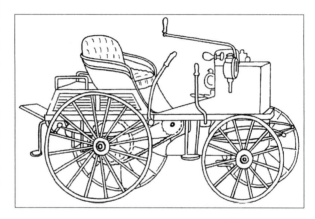

²Dog Cart. In this motorized Dog Cart the horse was replaced by an engine and front wheels.

the four-wheeled horse-drawn Dog Cart. Most had bench front and rear seats situated Dos-à-dos (back-to-back), each for two persons. There was no weather protection and most such vehicles had tiller steering. The engine was often located underneath, mid-chassis, but, as illustrated, a few advanced French designs sported front-mounted engines. Panhard & Levassor actually type-designated their Dog Cart "Dog-cart."

Doktor Coupé
German alternative term for Doctor's Coupé
→ *Doctor's Coupé*

Doktorwagen

German for Doctor's Coupé
→ *Doctor's Coupé*

Doppelphaeton

German for Double-Phaeton. This body style was common in Germany up to World War I, after which it was more or less replaced by the Tourenwagen (Touring Car).
→ *Double-Phaeton*

Doppio Phaéton

Italian for Double-Phaeton.
→ *Double-Phaeton*

[1]d'Orsay, Dorsay

According to Henri-Labourdette the rounded back form of the original 18th century horse-drawn Coupé was called Dorsay (*see illustration [1]Coach*). On the other hand, Coupé d'Orsay was a name applied after Count Alfred d'Orsay to a 19th century Coupé carriage, according to Sallmann, who also states that the rounded back of the Coupé body was not abandoned in favor of the stepped form until after 1870. This had to do with the different fixation to the carriage chassis under the rear part of the body of elliptic leaf springs of steel, which replaced the earlier strap suspension.

[2]d'Orsay, Dorsay

A comprehensive description of the various automobile bodyworks, made mainly in the 1920s by coachbuilders, which were accorded this name is hardly possible. Some were smaller Coupé style bodies, some were enclosed large vehicles, some were Convertible or Touring types. Only a very few did exhibit the rounded body curve that was a characteristic, and originated with the horse-drawn Coupé carriage. It must be assumed that the name in itself held an irresistible attraction to coachbuilders, which led to its manifold and incoherent uses.

Dos-à-dos

French for back-to-back. An open, very early and primitive four-seater motor vehicle having passenger benches usually on top of the body with the rear-seat passengers facing backwards. This type of seating had disappeared by 1900, but revivals have been attempted from time to time, notably the German mid-engined Zündapp Janus, produced 1957–1958, and the experimental (prototype) Swedish Volvo type

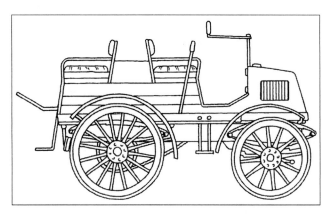

Dos-à-dos. This term describes only the seating arrangement of an early primitive automobile.

LCP, designed and built in the early 1980s. The latter was prompted partly to increase safety for the two rear seat passengers.

Language varieties

Dos-à-dos was an international term.

In America and Great Britain it was spelled Dos-a-dos.

Double Brougham

A Brougham horse-drawn carriage for four passengers.

→ *¹Brougham*

Double Phaeton

An open, rather sporting, Continental European Touring Car type of automobile having usually comfortable seating for five, and sometimes having two foldable extra seats. Typically, the front and rear seats were of identical design and, especially in early examples, the upholstery was of the buttoned variety. A much favoured bodywork style in France and in Germany up to the mid-twenties, the Double Phaeton was never chauffeur driven. Many early specimens had only one Victoria-style top for the rear passengers and no front doors. Later cars sported a simple, but fully extensible, foldable top, windshield and canvas peg-on side curtains for weather protection. There were no center pillars. By World War I the car had acquired the characteristics of the later period Double Phaetons, including the Torpedo-style cowl between engine room and windshield *(see Torpedo)* and

a more or less straight waist- or beltline along the body side.

Origins and history

Although the name originates from the Double Phaeton horse-drawn carriage, the progenitor of the Phaeton and Double Phaeton automobile body styles was the Tonneau. The name came into being at the time when the rear entrance into the Tonneau was no longer necessary and the front compartment with its side doors could be doubled for the rear compartment. The early Double Phaeton automobiles were characterized by the comfortable and plushy semi-baroque style seat design inherited from the Tonneau. In France and Italy, the Double Phaeton body style was more or less superseded by the Torpédo style coachwork when the seating became simpler and integrated with the bodywork and the body line from the top of the bonnet sides rearwards along the body waist-line became continuous, or almost continuous.

Tonneau ←

Important period

1905–1930

Variations

A few very early Double Phaetons did not have the long, single extendible top but two separate Victoria-style tops in tandem. Later coachbuilt bodies were in some instances designed with a second, crank-down windshield immediately behind the front seats plus occasional seats. Unlike the still later American Dual-cowl Phaeton *(q.v.)* the European Double Phaeton did not nor-

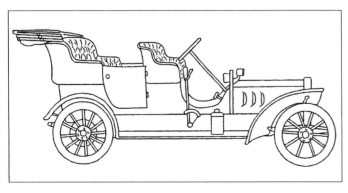

Double Phaeton. An early European Touring Car.

mally have a secondary cowl in front of the rear passenger compartment, or a secondary windshield, but this departure did exist in some coachbuilt European variations. Space taken by the rear cowl in these body styles limited passenger capacity to five. At least one European coachbuilding company, Labourdette of Paris, is known to have built in the early 1920s a couple of Double Phaetons with a secondary cowl and windshield plus a very original separate top for the rear passengers only. The same company constructed a Double Phaeton with a fifth rearmost central mechanic's seat behind the rear seats. The British vehicle corresponding to the Double Phaeton, both in purpose and general style, was the four- to seven-seater Tourer. It could be contended that the Triple Phaeton *(q.v.)* was an extended version of the Double Phaeton.

Language varieties

Despite the fact that Phaeton was a British name for some horse-drawn carriage types it appears that the name Phaeton/Double Phaeton was but seldom used in England for its motor propelled opposite number. On the Continent, some of the later straight-sided Phaetons were termed Torpedo Double Phaeton. In normal daily parlance, especially in France and in Italy, the Double Phaeton type of bodywork seems to have been abbreviated to just Phaéton. *See also Phaeton.*

American: Phaeton, Dual-cowl Phaeton.

British: Tourer.

French: Double Phaéton, Phaéton.

German: Doppelphaeton, Phaeton, Phaéton.

Italian: Doppio Phaéton, Double Phaéton, Phaéton.

→ *Dual-cowl Phaeton*

Dreirad
German for Tricycle.
→ *Tricycle*

Drei-Zellenstruktur
German technical term for Three-box or Notchback, alternative to Stufenheck.
→ *Notchback*

Dressurwagen
German for Brake.
→ *²Brake*

Drop-head Coupé (DHC)
British for a two to three seater Convertible Coupe.
→ *Convertible Coupe*

Drop-head Saloon
British for a four-door five to seven seater Convertible Sedan. Alternative term, favored by coachbuilders: Cabriolet.
→ *Convertible Sedan*

Drop-head Stretch-limousine
British for Convertible Stretch-limo.
→ *Convertible Stretch-limo*

¹Droschke
German for a horse-drawn carriage for hire.

Origins and history

The Russian term Drozjki derives from the shaft or pole of a wagon. The Drozjki was a light horse-drawn open carriage consisting of a simple four-wheeled chassis on which a body for passengers was suspended on leather straps. This original type of body was unusual in so far as it was divided and hung in two parts as low as possible on either side of the central chassis boom, allegedly in order to lower the vehicle's center of gravity. Two passengers could be seated on each side of the boom tunnel. In addition one more passenger could sit on the on top of the tunnel itself with legs on either side. In front was a driver's perch and at the rear a foldable top. Starting in the early 19th century the carriage came westward (and became known as Wurst in some Continental countries). As in so many other cases, the original carriage name Droschke was applied to modified vehicle types for the same purpose but without any resemblance to the original Russian carriage.

Drozjki ←

Important period

It is not clear when the original Russian Drozjki originated, but after having come westward in about 1800 it remained current during the whole century.

Variations

The Droschke name was even carried over to various motorized hire vehicles which eventually led to the contemporary Taxi.

Language varieties

Drosky and Droshky are anglicized terms of the Russian Drozjki.

→ *Fiacre 1*

²Droschke

An alternative German name, now obsolete, for a motor propelled Taxi in Germany and German-speaking parts of Switzerland. This term, with minor variations in spelling, could still be found in other European countries as late as during the second World War, when Taxi started to take over.

→ *Taxi*

Drozjki

Russian for a horse-drawn light carriage.

→ *Droschke*

Dual-cowl Phaeton

An open four-door American Touring Car type of automobile having comfortable seating for normally five passengers and a fully extensible, foldable top

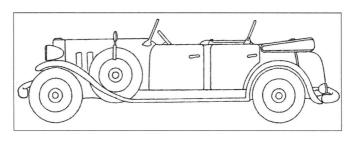

Dual-cowl Phaeton. A high-class American Touring Car variation.

and simple peg-on soft side windows. Almost without exception Dual-cowl Phaetons featured elegant, coachbuilt bodywork, usually on high-class chassis. Typical is the secondary cowl in front of the rear seat passengers which can be raised forward to facilitate entry to and egress from the rear seats, the tonneau. This cowl has almost always a tonneau windshield, which can be folded forward on to the cowl. No center posts. Seldom chauffeur driven. The Dual-cowl Phaeton was rarely an inexpensive car.

Origins and history

The Dual-cowl Phaeton grew out of the simpler, ubiquitous, Touring Car after World War I. A few examples are known from the late 1910s but this body style's real popularity started in the USA in the mid–1920s and continued well into the first half of the 1930s.

³*Phaeton;* ²*Touring Car* ←

Important period

1920–1933

Variations

A sporting touch was given some coachbuilt Dual-cowl Phaetons by cutting down the front doors or applying the name Dual-cowl Sport Phaeton. Some American standard production mid–1930s versions were built without the secondary cowl and windshield—these were in effect Touring Cars but were given the more prestigious Phaeton epithet. European Double Phaetons did not normally have a secondary cowl in front of the rear passenger compartment, or a secondary windshield, but this variation did exist in a few coachbuilt specimens *(see Double Phaeton)*.

Language varieties

Both Dual-cowl and non-dual-cowl Phaetons in America would sometimes be referred to simply as Phaetons. European Phaeton cars with or without secondary windshields in front of the rear seat passengers are termed, appropriately, Double Phaetons.

American: Dual-cowl Phaeton.
British: Double Phaeton.
French: Double Phaéton.
German: Doppelphaeton.
Italian: Doppio Phaéton, Double Phaéton.

Dual-cowl Sport Phaeton

A name applied by some American manufacturers to their high-performance coachbuilt Dual-cowl Phaeton automobiles.

→ *Dual-cowl Phaeton; Sports Tourer*

¹Duc

The Duc was a French horse-drawn carriage. There were two versions; a light four-wheeled open, elegant carriage driven from the passenger's seat and therefore without a front coachman's seat, and a heavier one with a coachman's perch in front. The lighter version was often preferred and driven by ladies. The passenger seat accommodated two persons and a Victoria-type folding top gave some shelter in bad weather. Some carriages had a rear Rumble seat for a footman (Sallmann).

Origins and history

The Duc carriage developed variously from similar vehicles, but one characteristic of the Duc was the ogee-shaped rearmost body wall ("ogee" is described in the Collins Dictionary as "a pointed arch having an S-shaped curve on both sides"). The later Duc carriages were fairly similar to the Phaeton.

Carrick ←

Important period

19th century.

Language varieties

British: Park phaeton, Ladies' Driving Phaeton.
German: Parkwagen.

²Duc

An open, rather primitive, usually two-seater motorized vehicle modeled more or less on the lines of the horse-drawn carriage by the same name. It had no doors but sometimes a folding top for weather protection. Sometimes it also had a Rumble seat.

Origins and history

Like so many other internal combustion engined early vehicles, the Duc's bodywork was patterned after the carriage body. The Duc automobile was a very French sort of vehicle.

¹Duc ←

Important period

1892–1908.

Variations

A lighter variation of this car was the French Petit Duc. With face-to-face seating an earlier variation of the Duc

was usually referred to as a Vis-à-vis (*q.v.*).
→ *Petit Duc; ²Phaeton*

Due volumi

Short for Carrozzeria a due volumi. Italian for Fastback.
→ *Fastback*

Dune Buggy

An American light, open, two-seater, usually rear-wheel driven motor vehicle adapted to be used off-road, fitted with simple doorless fiberglass bodywork, wide-rim wheels and oversize tires for traversing sand beaches without sinking in. This Buggy is almost always made out of the mechanical parts and platform-chassis (floorpan) of a Volkswagen.

Origins and history

The following are in part excerpts from *The Automobile* by Angelucci and

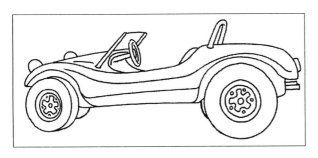

Dune Buggy. An American leisure vehicle based on European small car components.

Bellucci: The Dune Buggy, born in 1960, was the result of an attempt to develop new ideas for amusement. The United States, homeland of free time, has enormous sandy stretches in the California and Arizona deserts. A young Californian decided to make use of the sand dunes for a new kind of motorized amusement; with homemade tools he built a vehicle without a body, using the wrecks of a couple of Volkswagen "Beetles." The major changes consist of taking the body off a "Beetle" and shortening the platform base to about two meters length in order to render the necessary driving ease and light weight of the vehicle. Finally the above mentioned minimal bodywork is bolted on.

Beach Buggy ←
Important period
1960 to present.
Variations
There grew up a whole group of more sophisticated vehicles built with greater means and on the whole rather unfaithful to the original idea. The Dune Buggies produced industrially are too well-finished and refined to preserve the informal quality that made the first so popular with young people. They had lost some of their primitive charm and gained weight. N.b.: Buggy was a horse-drawn carriage in its own right—*see ¹Buggy* .
Language varieties
American: Dune Buggy.
British: Dune Buggy.
French: Buggy.
German: Buggy, Dune Buggy.
Italian: Dune Buggy.

-E-

E

This sub-type designation was initially employed by German car manufacturers to denote Einspritz (German for injection). E has also been used to indicate Executive (and perhaps Extra and Elegance), thus implying "luxury equipment" sometimes in combination with GL to form GLE. These designations reflect car manufacturers' desire to highlight the perceived value and status cachet of that particular model.

¹Electric Brougham

An American chauffeur-driven electric two-door automobile having an open chauffeur's seat separated from the enclosed two to four passenger compartment by a glass division, very much in the chauffeur-driven Brougham style *(see ²Brougham)*. These electrically propelled cars were in the United States consistently termed Brougham or Electric Brougham.

Origins and history
²Brougham ←
In the early years of the 1900s electricity was very much considered a viable proposition for propelling automobiles, there being in the United States more than 200 serious manufacturers of Electric Broughams. The number of makers of electric cars outside the United States was small in comparison.
Important period
1905–1915.
→ *²Electric Brougham*

²Electric Brougham

An American enclosed, inside-drive electrically propelled two-door automobile for four or five passengers with four or six side windows.

Origins and history
With the exception of the open-drive chauffeur's compartment, inside-drive Electric Broughams inherited the body style of the chauffeur-driven Electric Broughams.
¹Electric Brougham ←
Important period
1910–1925.
Variations
The transition of Brougham vehicles generally from being chauffeur-driven to becoming owner-driven happened approximately in the important period mentioned above. The inside-drive electric Brougham was a fairly rigid body style, but a few manufacturers did produce some larger four-door vehicles having Sedan and Limousine style bodies. Their heavier weight, however, must have considerably limited their usable range. The name Brougham be-

²Electric Brougham. When the early open-drive Electric Broughams became inside-drive the name stuck. The illustration shows an Electric Brougham from the period 1910–1915.

came subsequently and prolifically used by American auto manufacturers for internal combustion engined cars, up to ca. 1935.

→ *⁴Brougham*

Enclosed drive

American and British term for vehicles having a fully weather protected chauffeur's compartment in front of the glass division.

Language varieties

American: Enclosed drive, Inside drive.
British: Inside drive, Enclosed drive.
French: Conduite Intérieure
German: Innenlenker, Innensteuer.
Italian: Guida interna.

¹Estate Car

British for Station Wagon. A three- or five-door car based on the normal production Sedan but having the roof extended backwards to form an enclosed and spacious rear compartment, with a rear door usually hinged transversely at its upper edge. Seating capacity up to seven. The rear seats fold forward to increase the carrying space. Usually smaller than the American Station Wagon. For illustration, *see Station Wagon*.

Origins and history

The first examples of Estate Cars in Europe appeared in the late 1930s. Apart from limited production conversions into Estate Cars of vans, among the first British industrially produced cars of this kind were the Standard Vanguard and Austin Countryman. Other countries were quick to catch on.

⁴Brake; Station Wagon ←

Important period
1950s to present.

Variations

A Shooting Brake is a British luxuriously appointed Estate Car. The term originates from the times when a horse-drawn Break was used for shooting parties. A variation is the Estate Car with visible parts of the bodywork aft of the engine compartment manufactured of wood rather than sheet steel, in the United States after World War II popularly called Woodie. As early as the mid–1930s some wooden British Estate Cars were built, and in the 1950s quite a few used two-tone ersatz wood (plastic) strips along the rear flank to emulate the American Woodie *(q.v.)*.

Language varieties

Outside the British isles in Europe Kombi is a common way of denoting an Estate Car. Kombi was originally an abbreviation of the German Kombiwagen, signifying several uses combined in one vehicle. A practical variation of this body style is the short-roof Hatch-back Kombi-coupé (three-door) and the Kombi-sedan (five-door), which are more or less similar to two- and four-door Sedans but have a sloping rear door which includes the rear window, hinged transversely at its upper edge (liftback).

→ *Kombi-coupé; Kombi-sedan*

²Estate Car

Another Estate Car variety is the GT-Estate, a lighter, more sporting and usually expensive vehicle with an extended roof and never more than three doors.

→ *GT-Estate (GTE)*

-F-

Fahrgestell

German for Chassis.

→ *Chassis*

Familiale

Alternative French term for Station Wagon. Seating capacity usually in excess of six. By contrast, a Break *(q.v.)* is normally a similar vehicle with seating limited to six.

→ *Station Wagon*

Familiare

Italian for Station Wagon. Break and Station Wagon are alternative terms used in Italy. Promiscua is also a Station Wagon or Break but better suited for alternative goods transportation. By Giardinetta is meant a small Station Wagon. Monovolume is the large variation (see *Minivan*).

→ *Station Wagon*

Fastback

Originally an American term to describe a closed car bodywork having a slant back sloping in a continuous line from the roof to the rear extremity of the car. This term is sometimes and loosely used for any kind of car with a rearward sloping roof. Two-box (as opposed to Three-box or Notchback) is an alternative, more technically oriented, term. The rear spoiler in the form of a transverse wing, a contemporary fashion feature which is useful only sometimes, confuses the issue. On a Fastback style of bodywork the spoiler, fixed about midway, interrupts the slope. The spoiler is supposed to improve the car's behavior on the road at speed, but unfortunately does so only to some car models. The net effect is most often just a disturbed body outline.

Language varieties

American: Fastback, Two-box.

British: Fast-back, Two-box.

French: Panneau AR fuyant, Carrosserie deux volumes or Bicorps.

German: Fliessheck or Zwei-Zellenstruktur.

Italian: Carrozzeria a due volumi or Fast-back.

[1]Faux-cabriolet

French for a horse-drawn enclosed carriage for two passengers with a fixed roof simulating a foldable top.

[1]*Coupé* ←

[2]Faux-cabriolet

An enclosed two- or four-door Coupe automobile having a fixed metal top covered with weatherproof, painted fabric or synthetic material, sometimes even with ornamental exter-

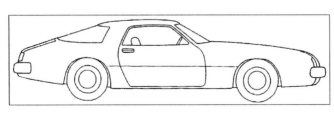

Fastback. An American two-door Fastback body style.

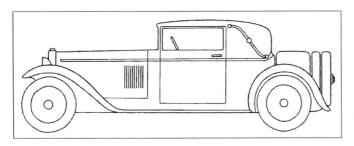

²**Faux-cabriolet. The European Faux-cabriolet was characterized by its outside dummy Landau bars.**

nal dummy Landau bars, designed to simulate a foldable Convertible top. Even one or two open-drive Town Cars are known to have been coachbuilt around 1930 displaying Landau bars. Unlike the original American Hardtop body style the Faux-cabriolet nowadays does not embody the disappearing B-pillars, but, interestingly, when American manufacturers after the mid–1970s introduced the pillared Hardtop coupé body style with a different roof construction the circle back to Faux-cabriolet became complete.

³*Coupé* ←

Important period
1920s to early 1950s.

Language varieties
American: Landau + Coupe/Sedan etc., later Hardtop.
British: Fixed-head Cabriolet.
French: Faux-cabriolet.
German: Faux-Cabriolet.
Italian: Faux-cabriolet.
→ ³*Cabriolet*

³Faux-cabriolet

In America, an example of a Faux-cabriolet, although not named thus, was the 1928 LaSalle two-passenger Coupe, complete with Landau bars. A fixed-roof two-door car simulating a Convertible is sometimes termed Hardtop Convertible, or occasionally even Victoria.
→ ¹*Hardtop*

FHC

(Fixed Head Coupé)
British for Coupé.
→ ³*Coupé*

¹Fiacre

A horse-drawn Fiacre, as we still know it today for the benefit of tourists, e.g. in Vienna, Austria, and Interlaken, Switzerland, is a four-wheeled open Victoria-style carriage with a folding top for the (rear-seat) passengers and an outside seat in front for the driver.

Origins and history
It is strongly assumed, and reported by many carriage historians, that the name Fiacre derives from the 6th century monk St. Fiacrius whose portrait adorned the 17th century Parisian house of Nicolaus Sauvage, the first to have offered horse-drawn carriages including driver for public hire.

Important period
Mid–17th century to World War I.

Language varieties
Robert Sallmann states that the original term Fiaker (Fiacre) does not constitute any particular type of carriage, but merely a carriage used for hire and different in type and style according to national preferences and time periods.
American: Cab.
British: Hackney carriage.
French: Fiacre.
German (Germany and part of Switzerland): Droschke.
German (Austria): Fiaker.
Italian: Fiacre, Vettura di Piazza.
→ *Droschke*

²Fiacre

In France, the first motor-propelled

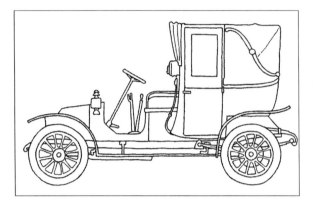

²Fiacre. The Fiacre was an early Continental Taxi.

German (Germany and part of Switzerland): Droschke.
German (Austria): Fiaker.
Italian: Automobile di Piazza.
→ Landaulet-Fiacre; Landaulet-Limousine; Taxi

Fiaker

German language version of Fiacre.
→ Fiacre

Fish-tail

Variant description of a Boattail style of bodywork.
→ Boattail

Five-door Hatchback

British for Hatchback Sedan.
→ Hatchback Sedan

Fixed-head Cabriolet

British for a Faux-cabriolet.
→ ²Faux-cabriolet

Fixed-head Coupé (FHC)

British for a two to three seater Coupe car.
→ ³Coupé

taxis were called Fiacres. Early specimens of these had a two-seater rear compartment for passengers. There were both enclosed as well as rear Quarter semi-open Landaulet passenger compartments. The driver's seat was quite open, but, as illustrated, he could unfold forward a small hood to fend off rain. The Landaulet bodywork appears to have been the most commonly used style.

Origins and history

As is the case with many early motorized vehicles, the form is based closely on that of the earlier horse-drawn carriage.
¹Fiacre ←

Important period
1905–1915.

Variations

Later the driver was to acquire both windshield and roof. Some of these vehicles sported a fixed roof rack for passenger luggage.

Language varieties

The Landaulet style of Fiacres were sometimes referred to as Landaulet-Fiacres. Apparently, this style of Landaulet was termed Single Landaulet in England.
French: Fiacre, Cab.

Flattop

An informal term applied originally by American enthusiasts to describe the roof and panoramic rear screen of a particular Hard-top Sedan bodywork style, having the roof extended backwards beyond the top of the rear window. There were no D-pillars, and usually no B-pillars. The rear window glass was wrapped all the way between the C-pillars.

Origins and history

An American bodywork style introduced in the late 1950s by some American and one European marque. Flat-

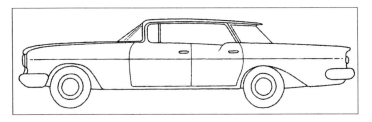

Flattop. This term, for an extended rear roof design, was never applied by car manufacturers.

top is a colloquial term, never used officially by the auto manufacturers.
    Important period
1959.
→ *¹Hardtop*

Fliessheck
    German for Fastback.
→ *Fastback*

Floorpan
    Floorpan is contemporary British English for the horizontal steel construction which forms the basis for attaching the engine, drive line, suspension, steering, bodywork etc. on which the car is built up integrally into one unit.
    American: Platform.
    British: Floorpan.
    French: Plate-forme.
→ *Platform*

Folding Head DHC
    Term used by some car makers to describe a soft top which could be placed in a semi-open position, with the front part of the hood folded and the rear part erect, Victoria style, thus covering only the rear seats. Alternative term: Three-position Drop-head Coupé.
→ *Cabriolet-victoria*

4x4/Four-by-four
    4x4 is used by some manufacturers of four-wheel drive cars as a subtype des-

ignation to indicate that all four wheels of a four-wheeled vehicle are either permanently engaged (driven) or that, usually, the front wheels can be disengaged at the driver's discretion. Before front-wheel drive became shortened as fwd, the initials FWD used to denote four-wheel drive.
→ *Off-roader*

Four-door Drop-head Limousine
    British for a long open Limousine with capacity for six or seven passengers.
→ *Pullman-Kabriolett*

Fourgonnette
    A derivative of the French Forgon, which was a horse-drawn carriage for goods. Fourgonnette is an alternative French name for Station Wagon, with some lingering commercial vehicle connotations.
→ *⁴Break; Station Wagon*

Four-light/ Four-light Saloon
    British for a Sedan with, usually, a short roof and always four side windows. A Four-light Saloon is not necessarily Close-coupled *(q.v.)*.

4WD/Four Wheel Drive
    Variant term for 4x4/Four-by-four.
→ *Off-roader*

"Full" Landaulet
    There is no difference between an early chauffeur-driven Cabriolet and a Full Landaulet. The term is futile, but

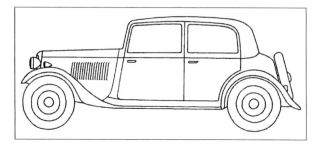

Four-light Saloon. A typical mid–1930s British Saloon having four side windows.

apparently came about when the Landaulet (with a collapsible head over the rear Quarter) was a more common body style than the Cabriolet, as described under ²*Cabriolet.*

→ ²*Cabriolet;* ²*Landaulet*

Fuoristrada

Italian for a four-wheel drive cross-country car. (Colloquially sometimes used also for an SUV type of vehicle, but not strictly correct.)

→ *Off-roader*

FWD

FWD, or fwd, in today's parlance, means front-wheel drive. It used to mean four-wheel drive (4WD). (Note: there is an American manufacturer of four-wheel drive commercial vehicles by the name of FWD Auto Co.)

-G-

Gala Coach

A heavy and luxurious horse-drawn ceremonial Coach for state or gala occasions. Designs vary.

Carrozza ←

Galawagen

German for Gala Coach. Alternative to Prachtwagen.

Carrozza ←

Geländewagen

German for a four-wheel-drive cross-country vehicle.

→ *Off-roader*

Gestreckte Limousine

Formal alternative in German for Stretch-limousine.

→ *Stretch-limo*

Giardinetta

Italian for a small Station Wagon. Familiare, Break or Station Wagon means the normal European size Station Wagon.

→ *Familiare; Station Wagon*

Giardiniera

Italian for an early gardener's two- or four-wheeled cart. This term was also used to denote an elegant, open four-wheeled gentleman's horse-drawn carriage. When used today, the term actually means a Giardinetta.

→ *Giardinetta*

GL

The GL subtype designation, for Grand Luxe, is a classic which manufacturers started to use as early as in the

1920s. Delage in France applied it to one of their chassis in that period, whereas later, when automobile manufacturers started to make the complete vehicle including bodywork, it became often applied as a subtype designation to the car's model name. This popular epithet has been used after World War II for car models which have rarely been particularly luxurious.

Glass Quarter Brougham

A large Brougham having windows in the rear Quarters (British: Quarterlights). Opposite of Panel Brougham.

→ *Limousine Brougham*

GLE

For the "GL" part, *see GL* above. The additional E became applied after World War II in some cases intended to mean Executive, in some others meaning Extra or Elegance, in an effort to further augment the feeling of luxury. (Inquiries with car manufacturers reveal that they seem to have applied these initials arbitrarily and without attaching any significance to them.) Car manufacturers in German speaking countries have used E to indicate injection (Einspritz).

→ *E; GL*

Goutte d'eau

French for a teardrop body style, flowing down to the rear (The Classic Car Club of America).

GR

French car manufacturers which in recent decades have used this subtype designation for some quite small normal family cars may have misguidedly had Grande Routière in mind.

→ *Grande Routière*

Grande Routière

Grande Routière is French for a two-door Convertible automobile with ample space for luggage for making fast long-distance journeys in comfort and elegance. Usually this style of bodywork is open and has comfortable seats for just the driver and one passenger, but some were provided with two additional rear seats or one only, which was designed for crosswise seating and was sometimes removable. The open Grande Routière had a high quality top and tight shutting windows and window frames. A Grande Routière was normally coach-

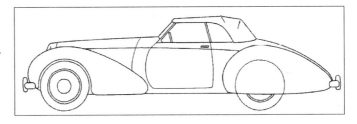

Grande Routière. A French Grande Routière could be an open Cabriolet style automobile or a Coupé (enclosed).

built on a fairly large and expensive French chassis. The wheelbase may sometimes be shorter than that of a large French Berline (Sedan) of otherwise roughly similar external proportions.

Origins and history

Between World Wars I and II the requirement arose for essentially two affluent people to travel long distances in comfort. French coachbuilders provided vehicles in the form of the (usually) folding top Grande Routière. There were national departures—*see Variations* below.

Important period

Around 1930 to the 1950s.

Variations

Excellent possibilities for studying Grande Routière designs from different countries were offered at the yearly European Auto Shows in the 1930s, but perhaps more so at the popular *Concours d'Élégance* contests both before and after World War II. Variations included Continental Coupés, enclosed Gran Turismos and some Cabriolet-victorias.

→ *Cabriolet-victoria;* [1, 2]*Gran Turismo*

Grand Sport

French variation of Sports Tourer, sometimes also applied to open pukka Sports Cars. Abbreviation: GS.

→ *Sports Tourer*

Grand Sport Torpédo

French for Sports Tourer in the 1920s; later termed just Grand Sport. Abbreviation: GS.

→ *Sports Tourer*

Grand Tourer

British for Gran Turismo (GT). A two-door fixed-head or drop-head automobile with amenities for two people to travel long distances in comfort and luxury, with good facilities for carrying luggage. Often has two extra rear seats and bodywork adapted to carry two spare wheels. Comfort and elegance were the hallmark for touring in the grand manner. The bodywork was often of considerable beauty. The Bentley Continental was a typical British Grand Tourer *(see Continental Coupé).* (N.b.:

A few coachbuilders mainly in the 1930s did construct some four-door Continentals.)

→ *Gran Turismo*

Grand Touring

American for Gran Turismo.

→ *Gran Turismo*

Grand Tourisme

French for Gran Turismo (GT). Alternative term: Voiture Grand Tourisme.

→ *Gran Turismo*

Gran Sport

Italian for Sports Tourer. Gran Sport has also sometimes been applied to open pukka Sports Cars. An earlier variation was the Torpedo Gran Sport. Abbreviation: GS.

→ *Sports Tourer*

[1]Gran Turismo (GT)

Italian, internationally renowned and used designation for a two-door, essentially fixed-head (Coupé), automobile with amenities for two people to travel long distances fast in comfort, with the bodywork adapted to provide good facilities for carrying luggage, fuel and, earlier, two spare wheels. Originally in the 1930s there were two extra and usually less comfortable rear seats for two passengers but in recent years the GT is sometimes designed as a four-seater car. Comfort, elegance and performance are the hallmarks for touring in the grand manner. The bodywork is often of considerable beauty. GT cars have very seldom been built in large series; before World War II they were the prerogative of the special coachbuilder. The wheelbase may differ from that of a normal Sedan of otherwise roughly similar external proportions. The engine does not have to be extremely powerful

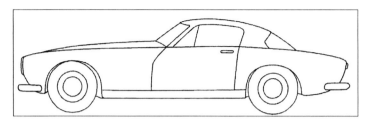

[1]Gran Turismo. A Gran Turismo automobile is always enclosed, Coupé style.

(although rather pointless suggestions to the opposite have been put forward from time to time). With beauty of bodywork, which used to be quite heavy, the GT hands nobly over to the Coupé and the Berlinetta the advantages of utility.

Origins and history

Between World Wars I and II the requirement arose for essentially two affluent people to be able to travel long distances in comfort. For this purpose, small, specialized automobile factories and coachbuilders provided an expensive version of an essentially Coupe-style vehicle in the form of the enclosed Gran Turismo automobile.

[3]Coupé ←

Important period

Around 1930 to the present day.

Variations

A British variation of Grant Turismo is Continental Coupé, whereas the French interpretation is the Grande Routière. Although a powerful engine is not a criterion some large, very powerful and comfortable post–World War II closed Supercars of limited production can be considered modern equivalents of the Gran Turismo. The type designation GTO, where O stands for omologato (Italian for homologated, meaning that a manufacturer has proved that their race car has been produced in a stipulated minimum number

to comply with a race regulation) was applied initially as an unofficial type designation to one Ferrari model, and in the mid–1960s as a subtype designation to two American Muscle Cars, a two-door Hardtop and a Convertible Pontiac Tempest Le Mans (see Muscle Car). (The denomination Gran Turismo Coupé can be seen sometimes, but this is a perfectly unnecessary designation, since Gran Turismo implies enclosed Coupé-style bodywork.)

Language varieties

American: Grand Touring, Gran Turismo or GT.

British: Continental Coupé, Grand Tourer.

French: Grand Tourisme or Grande Routière.

German: Reise-Coupé, Autobahn Kurier, Gran Turismo.

Italian: Gran Turismo.

→ Supercar

[2]Gran Turismo (GT)

An alternative term in French fulfills almost all of the above criteria is Grande Routière. However, whereas the GT is always closed, the Grande Routière can also be an open, luxurious convertible.

→ Grande Routière

[3]Gran Turismo (GT)

The initials GT have unfortunately been used loosely since about 1963 as a model subtype designation for all kinds of cars, and in the 1980s and 1990s even for some racing formulæ.

Gran Turismo Internazionale

Full name of the internationally used, originally Italian, subtype designation GTi or GTI.

Greenhouse

American for upper part of the passenger's compartment or cabin; the structure above the body waistline or beltline—glass, roof and supporting members (Dick Nesbitt). Alternative term: Top (which can also be construed as a foldable hood). Greenhouse or Top implies a horizontal division of the body, instead of the vertical one indicated by Box *(q.v.)*. Greenhouse has been incorporated in some European car manufacturers' non–English company vocabulary.

Top ←

GS

French-Italian model subtype designation with a provenance. Used carelessly by some car manufacturers for various and mostly quite non-sporting car types, the initials GS correctly imply Sports Tourer. The GS designation has also sometimes been used for Sports Cars.

→ *Gran Sport; Grand Sport*

GT

A classical abbreviation of Gran Turismo and Grand Tourisme/Touring, meaning a comfortable Coupé-style automobile for long-distance travel. Applied after World War II abundantly and seldom quite correctly as a subtype designation to normal Sedans and other non–Gran Turismo–like products. GT has also been used arbitrarily since ca. 1960 for various race categories to cover two-seater and even Sedan cars for racing, often in much modified form. The inclusion of these initials in race category names may, in part, explain the reasons for their extensive use as subtype designations for non-race cars. For the initials GTO, *see* ¹*Gran Turismo.*

Gran Turismo ←

GTE

Reliant in Great Britain initiated GTE as subtype designation for one of their models. These initials have since been found very practical to use in some countries as an abbreviation for the GT-Estate bodywork style.

→ *GT-Estate*

GT-Estate

A modern, usually more sporting and exclusive variation of the European Estate Car. There are three doors only; a hatchback-type rear door opens Liftback style with rear window. The abbreviated designation GTE is often used. This body style was successfully launched by Reliant with their Scimitar and has since been perpetuated by Volvo, Gilbern, Jensen, Lancia and some other manufacturers.

French: Coupé break.

³*Estate Car* ←

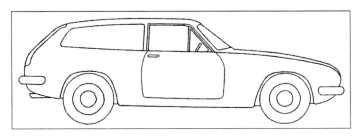

GT-Estate. A European three-door classy style of Estate Car.

GTi

A number of small, sporting and agile Three-door Hatchbacks have in the most recent decades been subdesignated GTi, the Italian abbreviation for Gran Turismo Internazionale. Although the GT part of this designation, in most cases, is not entirely appropriate, the "i" part is quite so. The GTi vehicle has proved an eminently practical car for the young sporting family man, but equally suitable for the sporting senior gentleman who does not need something grandiose for his enclosed car requirements. Hot Hatch is a colloquial British name for this type of vehicle.

→ *GT; I; Ti*

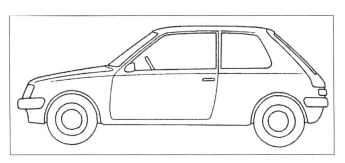

GTi. A small, sporty Hot Hatch.

Guida interna

Italian, literally, for Inside drive—a term to indicate that the chauffeur's compartment in front of the glass division is fully weather protected.

-H-

Hack

Colloquial British term for a horse for hire, a taxi or a second-hand and not much cared-for car, usually a Sedan or pick-up vehicle used for any kind of errand. This term is an abbreviation of Hackney *(q.v.)*.

Hackney ←

¹Hackney

English for a compact breed of harness horse with a high-stepping trot or a horse kept for riding. Hackney derives from French "hacquence" for hired horses (Robertson).

²Hackney

A carriage or coach for hire, the legal name of which was—in England—Hackney carriage. One style of horse-drawn vehicle that became later used in the Hackney trade was the Clarence, colloquially known as Growler.

→ *Clarence; Taxi*

Hackney Coach

→ *²Hackney*

Halbberline

German for a "half-Berline"; i.e., a late 17th century Berline carriage with the front part cut off so as to make space for two passengers only.

→ *¹Coupé*
¹Berline ←

¹Hansom Cab

A two-wheeled, one-horse carriage having an enclosed compartment for passengers, purpose-built for public

Hansom Cab. A very early form of "Taxi!"

hire including driver. The driver's seat was elevated at the rear. The abbreviation Cab was used in English speaking countries as well as in France and Italy.

Origins and history
Patented by the architect J. A. Hansom in England in 1834 and further developed and improved by others, the Hansom Cab, replacing the Hackney, became popular in London and other British cities, but also (according to Sallmann) in New York and Berlin. In London some were still in use at the beginning of the Second World War.

Hackney ←

Important period
Almost a hundred years, starting in the 1830s.

²Hansom Cab
A motor propelled taxi-cab utilizing the horse-drawn Hansom Cab style bodywork with the driver sitting behind and above the passenger compartment.

Origins and history
The horseless Hansom Cabs were modeled after their horse-drawn predecessor. The earliest one appears to have been the electrically propelled French Hautier built in 1898. In 1899 Illinois Electric produced a rear-wheel steered variation, and, before World War I, also

Riker, Woods and Columbia in the United States made some electrically propelled taxicabs of this type. In England, Vauxhall built an experimental internal combustion driven specimen in 1905, as did coachbuilder J.H. Labourdette in France, as late as 1946. None of the motor driven Hansom Cabs seemed to have approached the popularity of their horse-drawn ancestor.

Important period
No important period because of experimental and sporadic production.

→ *Taxi*

¹Hardtop/Hard-top
Hardtop was originally an American abbreviation for Hardtop Convertible, meaning a two- or four-door car having the special characteristic of no B-pillar but a fixed metal roof imitating the soft, folding canvas top of a Convertible car. The head is fixed but is made to look like it could be folded down. The true pillarless design was a feature in the United States until about 1977; thereafter pillared versions continued to be made by some manufacturers, still termed Hardtop, especially if the top was or appeared to be made of a different material from the main body.

Origins and history
The idea to produce the Hardtop style may have sprung from the pre–World War II French Faux-cabriolet body style, which was not, however, notable for a disappearing B-pillar effect. The first Hardtops proper were produced in the early 1950s and the style was applied to both two-door and four-

door bodywork variations, and even to some Station Wagons. Particularly in the United States, Hardtop used to imply that the front and rear side windows met without a (B-) pillar, but by 1976–77 American car producers, facing rollover standards, had turned away from the pillarless design to pillared versions (Flammang & Kowalke).

Hardtop Convertible ←

Important period
1950 to the mid–1980s.

Variations
In 1917 Hudson produced a Sedan having both B- and C-pillars removable, thereby creating in effect an early "Hardtop"-looking automobile. It is doubtful, however, if the intention was to make the roof look removable. A vehicle that could be construed as an early Hardtop was the American Westcott Model B-44 "permanent top" Touring Car of 1923. Some ordinary fixed top Sedan cars sported already in the 1920s dummy external Landau bars, apparently as a decoration but without the express intention to simulate a foldable top. General Motors in the mid–1970s introduced the term Colonnade for their essentially two-door pillared Hardtops, according to Flammang & Kowalke, with arch-like rear Quarter windows and sandwich type roof construction. It would seem that this body style in fact turned back to the style intentions of the original French Faux-cabriolet coachwork. A special Hardtop roof design was the Flattop *(q.v.)*.

Language varieties
Hard-top or Hardtop is nowadays an internationally used term. In some French and German speaking countries Faux-cabriolet is still used as an alternative to Hard-top. Some American

high-class two-door Hardtop bodied cars have been called Victoria *(q.v.)*.
American: Hardtop.
British: Hard-top.
French: Hardtop, Faux-cabriolet.
German: Hardtop, Hardtop-Limousine.
Italian: Hard-top, Vettura a tetto rigido.
→ *Faux-cabriolet*

[2]Hardtop/Hard-Top
A separate, removable top made of metal, fiberglass or some hard material that can be fitted to a small Convertible, a Sports Car (usually a two-seater) or a smallish three-door SUV. The removable hardtop is often an accessory that can be purchased from aftermarket suppliers rather than the car manufacturer. A pre-World War II counterpart was the All-year Top.

Language varieties
American: Hardtop Coupe (removable).
British: Hard-top Coupé (removable).
French: Hardtop Coupé (amovible).
German: Hardtop Coupé/Kupee (entnehmbar).
Italian: Hard-top (amovibile).
→ *All-year Top;* [2]*Coupé Cabriolet*

[1]Hardtop Convertible
The original American term for a two- or four-door American automobile having a fixed roof without a B-pillar to imitate a Convertible body style.
→ [1]*Hardtop 1*

[2]Hardtop Convertible
Modern American term for a two- or four-seater open two-door car with a retractable hard metal roof which, with power assistance, can be folded and stowed into the trunk, thereby making

it in effect a Convertible car. With the roof closed the top is well insulated and the external visual impression is that of a fully enclosed Coupe.

→ ²*Coupé-cabriolet*

Hardtop Coupe

American term to specify a two-door Hardtop Coupé style of car.

→ ¹*Hardtop*

Hardtop-Limousine

German for Hardtop.

→ ¹*Hardtop*

Hardtop Sedan

American term to specify a two- or four-door Hardtop Sedan car.

→ ¹*Hardtop*

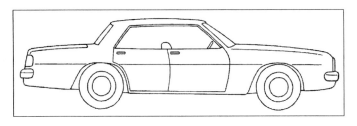

Hardtop Sedan. An American Hardtop, here the old genuine style without B-pillars.

¹Hatchback

American and British for a three- or five-door variation (i.e. two- or four-door vehicles with a Fastback rear hatch) of an essentially Coupe or Sedan bodywork style. The roof length rearwards is the criterion: A car with an extended roof is a full Station Wagon whereas the Hatchback has the normal two- or four-door car's shorter roof and a large, more or less sloping (Fastback) rear hatch that includes the rear window. In some bodywork designs the rear hatch is of the Notchback style.

Origins and history

The idea of opening a rear gate or door goes far back in time. Charabancs and early chain-drive Touring Cars had a rear central door for entry and egress to the rear seats, although for a different reason *(see Rear-entrance Tonneau),* and the classic Station Wagon, of course, had a tailgate. The first post–World War II vehicles of the normal roof, Fastback-Hatchback bodywork style had a slow start. The initial American models were based on four-door Sedans in the early 1950s, but weather-tightness was a problem (Flammang & Kowalke). In Europe Citroën in France were first to introduce in the mid–1950s their Commerciale *(q.v.)* with a full Hatchback door, but it was not until the mid–1960s that the Renault type 16 followed, which really set in motion the Hatchback trend in Europe. These American and European pioneers were eventually followed by a multitude of both small and larger Hatchback designs, which continue to enjoy great popularity.

Language varieties

Especially the Fastback rear hatch style was in earlier parlance sometimes referred to as Liftback (Lift-back). In some Continental European and Nordic countries this type of bodywork is often spoken of as Kombi-coupé (three-door) or Kombi-sedan (five-door).

→ *Hatchback Coupe; Hatchback Sedan*

²Hatchback

A car's sloping rear end consisting of a large door which includes the rear window and is hinged transversely at the top.

Hatchback Coupe

A three-door variation of a two-door Coupe. The normal Coupe roof length is the criterion (a car with an extended roof is a Station Wagon). The Hatchback bodywork is characterized by the normal car's short roof, a large rear hatch which is more or less sloping, Fastback style *(q.v.),* or sometimes Notchback style *(q.v.),* usually hinged transversely at its upper edge (Liftback). There is no separate trunk. The luggage carrying capacity can be augmented by collapsible or removable rear seats to achieve an extended and fairly large floor area.

Origins and history
For origins, refer to *¹Hatchback.*
Important period
Early 1960s to present.

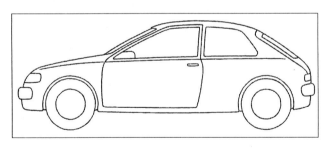

Hatchback Coupe. The Hatchback Coupe is in principle a two-door Sedan with a rear liftback hatch.

Variations
Some modern, compact three-door Hatchback Coupe cars—especially in the small size favored in the far East and some parts of Europe—have bodyworks employing a roof and hatch form that could make then difficult to distinguish from small three-door Station Wagons. Usually, the rear overhang is very short as compared to the more normal-sized Hatchback Sedan. A number of small sporting vehicles of the Hatchback Coupé style have in recent decades been subdesignated GTi and established themselves as a class of vehicle in their own right (GTi being the Italian abbreviation for Gran Turismo Internazionale—*see GTi*). A rather sporting and usually more refined variation of the Hatchback Coupé is the (three-door) GT-Estate *(q.v.).*

Language varieties
In some Continental European and the Nordic countries this type of bodywork is often rendered as Kombi-coupé *(q.v.).*

American: Two-door/Three-door Hatchback Coupe.
British: Three-door Hatchback.
French: Berline à 3 portes.
German: Kombi-Limousine, dreitürig.
Italian: Berlina 3-porte.
➙ *GT-Estate; GTi; Hatchback Sedan*

Hatchback Sedan

A five-door variation of a four-door Sedan. The normal Sedan roof length rearwards is the criterion. (A car with an extended roof is a full Station Wagon.) The Hatchback has the normal car's short roof and a large, sloping Fastback (two-box) or sometimes Notchback (three-box) rear hatch, usually hinged transversely at its upper edge (Liftback), and a fairly large cargo capacity augmented by collapsible or removable rear seats to achieve an extended floor area.

Origins and history
For origins, refer to *¹Hatchback.*

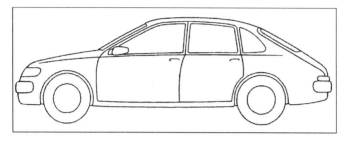

Hatchback Sedan. The Hatchback Sedan is a four-door Sedan with a fifth rear "door."

Important period
1950s to present.
Variations
The Hatchback Sedan's three-door correlative is the Hatchback Coupe. Because of their roof and hatch form and very short rear overhang, in the case of some small modern five-door hatchback cars manufactured outside the United States, it can be difficult—and perhaps meaningless—to determine whether they are small Station Wagons or Hatchback Sedans.
Language varieties
In some Continental European and the Nordic countries this type of bodywork is often referred to as Kombi-sedan *(q.v.)*.
American: Four-door/Five-door Hatchback Sedan.
British: Five-door Hatchback.
French: Berline à 5 portes.
German: Kombi-Limousine, fünftürig.
Italian: Berlina 5-porte.
→ *Hatchback Coupe*

Hearse
Funeral carriage or automobile for carrying a coffin to the grave or church. Cultures and traditions vary, but normally the auto chassis and front parts of the body are based on a long wheelbase series produced Sedan or van with the addition of coachbuilt rear bodywork. It is suitably appointed and externally lacquered in a color proper to the spirit of its use and according to national traditions and preferences.
Origins and history
The Hearse in its various carriage forms has been with us more or less since the advent of the wheeled wagon. Until World War II the use of horse-drawn Hearses at funerals was common.
Important period
(Motorized Hearses) From the 1950s to present.
Variations
The fundamental and singular pur-

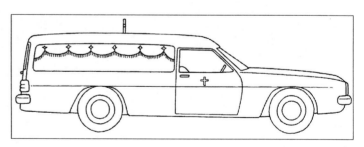

Hearse. A funeral vechicle, here an American-sized one.

pose of the Hearse has led to variations only in divine decorations and external size. However, teenage surfing youth in the United States have discovered in used Hearses the ideal transport for their boards and girlfriends.

Language varieties
American: Hearse.
British: Hearse.
French: Char funèbre, Corbillard.
German: Bestattungswagen, Leichen-
wagen.
Italian: Carro funebre.

High-wheeler

An American very early, light four-
wheeled automobile, having rudimentary two- or four-seater quite open
bodywork, usually tiller steering and a
simple foldable top. Very high and slim
wheels, typically of excellent quality,
were fitted with thin, solid rubber tires.

Origins and history

The earliest High-wheelers were constructed on the same lines as their predecessor horse-drawn Buggies. The

High-wheeler. A significant early American automobile.

Holsman Automobile Company was
one of the most successful producers of
High-wheelers between 1903 and 1910
inclusive, but there were many other
makes. This type of automobile was especially popular in the Midwest region
of the United States and well adapted to
the rough roads of the period. The contemporary Ford model T, as Oliver
notes, as well as the Jeep and Land

Rover, followed the same utilitarian
pattern. The obvious successors to the
High-wheelers were the early Runabouts.
¹Buggy ←

Important period

From 1896 to ca. 1915.

Variations

There were at least 250 manufacturers
of High-wheelers in the United States,
and the design varieties were innumerable. The usual pattern was a central
perch with an underseat engine, but at
least one is known to have been designed
for six passengers, four of them sitting
back-to-back. For propulsion there were
as a rule gasoline motors, but also steam
engines and electric motors. Other variations included chain drive, friction
drive, wire-spoke wheels, and three road
wheels. Many were one-
offs based on bicycle
parts; however, those that
were manufactured on a
series production basis
were sometimes provided
with wheel steering and
pneumatic tires.

Language varieties

Also known as Buggy,
Auto-Buggy, Motor
Buggy. One manufacturer
is known to have termed
his version "High-
wheeled Runabout."

→ *²Runabout*

Hofkutsche

German alternative for Prachtwagen.
Carrozza ←

Hot Hatch/Hothatch

Colloquial name for a small, sporting
Hatchback Coupe *(q.v.).* See also GTi.
GTi ←

Hot Rod

An American open, usually two-seater car manufactured by enthusiasts from various standard car and bodywork components at their own discretion, traditionally using a 1920s–30s chassis and bodywork combined with a considerably later engine, drive-line and road wheels. The typical Hot Rod is based on Ford chassis parts.

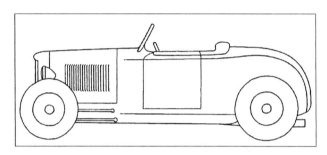

Hot Rod. An American enthusiast's very special Special.

Origins and history

The youthful enthusiasm for building one's own sporting vehicle, or Special, started with young men in the United States when the ubiquitous Ford model T became available as a cheap second-hand car in the third decade of the 20th century. In the 1930s the term "Hot rodding" was coined and in the following decades it became an organized movement.

Important period

1930s to the present time.

Variations

The Hot Rod developed along two distinct lines: one consisting of cars extensively modified and usually beautifully appointed and licensed for road use, the other for racing. In the 1930s the Hot Rod started to be built specifically for speed trials which became organized by the late 1930s in various classes depending on power-to-weight ratio, degrees of "hotting up" and modification. In its most extreme form the speed Hot Rod eventually became the 1/4-mile Dragster classified as Drag roadsters, Lakesters, Streamliners etc.

-I-

¹i

Short for "Internazionale." A classical and significant lower-case abbreviation, used as a subtype designation to indicate a vehicle's hoped-for attraction to an international and sporting range of customers.

Origins and history

Italian. Originally used in the 1950s by Italian car manufacturers, especially Alfa Romeo. Thereafter intermittently applied to some Continental European automobile makes, notably BMW. So far this designation seems to have been assigned primarily to smaller European Sedan cars with sporting aspirations (seating capacity up to five).

Important period

Intermittently from just after World War II to the present day.

Variations

Capital "I" is an alternative abbreviation. In either lower or uppercase form, "I" has been used immediately following a model type numeral, but more often in conjunction with "T" to form the model subtype designation Ti or TI *(q.v.)*.

²i

Short for (fuel) injection.

Origins and history

Diesel engines have always relied on some kind of fuel injection system. When gasoline engines lost their traditional carburetor based fuel system in favor of fuel injection it became important to announce this fact. Using the "i" subtype designation was one method.

Important period

Shortly after World War II to present.

Variations

Capital "I" is an alternative abbreviation. The "i" or "I" initial has been used in combinations, e.g. by Fiat as i.d. to signify direct injection (iniezione diretta). (Note: In German the abbreviation for fuel injection is E.)

Language varieties

American: Injection.
British: Injection.
French: Injection.
German: Einspritz.
Italian: Iniezione.

I

An abbreviation for "Internazionale,"

but also for "Injection," used as a sub-type designation. *See ²i.*

Origins and history

Italian. The original abbreviation was "i" for Internazionale—*see ¹i.* The capital "I" designation has been applied by manufacturers as a sub-type designation for both "Internazionale" and "Injection."

Important period

Shortly after World War II to present, in occasional use.

Variations

Often combined with "T" to form the model sub-type designation TI (or Ti) *(q.v.)* or with GT to form GTI or GTi *(q.v.)*.

Innenlenker

German, literally, for inside steering —a term to indicate a non-chauffeur-driven automobile. The term could equally mean a small Coupé or similar car never intended to be chauffeur-driven, as it is virtually synonymous with Owner-driver.

Innensteuer

German variant term for Innenlenker *(q.v.)*.

Inside drive

Variant term for Enclosed drive *(q.v.)*.

-J-

Jagdwagen
German for Shooting Brake.

→ *Shooting Brake*

Jeep

An American, originally military, four-wheel drive cross-country vehicle with basic open bodywork and usually simple means of weather protection. Several theories exist about the origins

Jeep. The original, stark military-bodied scout and reconnaissance car.

of the term; according to a popular one, which may not be correct, it derives from the abbreviation "GP" for General Purpose (vehicle). After World War II both open and enclosed civilian variations have been produced. Conceptually similar vehicles have also been made in quite a few other countries. The name Jeep should not be used to describe this kind of vehicle, as Jeep is a trademark belonging (today) to Daimler-Chrysler. Incidentally, also the seven-slot Jeep air intake grille is a trademark of the Daimler-Chrysler group.

→ *Off-roader*

Jump seat

American alternative for Rumble seat.

→ *Rumble seat*

-K-

K

The sub-type designation K has been employed by mainly German manufacturers to indicate "Kurz," for short wheelbase, the consequent bodywork

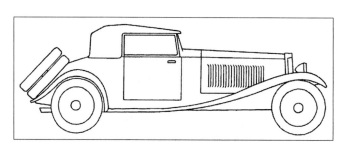

K. A German short-wheelbased vehicle was sometimes subtype designated K, for short.

shortening mostly taking place *behind* the engine compartment. A German car having this sub-type designation has usually sporting pretensions.

Kabinenroller

German for a Microcar of the immediate post–World War II era, most of which were Three-wheelers.

English: Bubblecar.

→ *Microcar; Tricar*

Kabriolett

Correct but somewhat archaic German

spelling of Cabriolet. Both terms mean fundamentally a four-door open automobile for about five passengers. Kabriolett in combination with another body style term usually indicates a car not having four doors.

→ *Convertible Sedan*

Kabriolett 3-Positionen Dach

German for Convertible Victoria in the 1920s and 1930s.

→ *Cabriolet-victoria*

Kabrio-Limousine

Variant, and probably original, spelling of the German Cabrio-Limousine.

→ *Cabrio-Limousine*

Kalesche

German for Calèche.

→ *Calèche*

Karosse

German alternative for Prachtwagen. (N.b. Not to be confused with Karosserie, which means bodywork/coachwork.)

Carrozza ←

Karosserie

German for Bodywork.

→ *²Bodywork*

King of Belgium

See Roi des Belges.

Kit Car

A usually open two-seater sporting car or Sports Car, sometimes in three-wheeler form, built by an enthusiast from parts manufactured industrially and supplied in kit form. The bodywork and interior fitments of such a vehicle are mostly simple and spartan.

Kleinbus

German for Minibus.

→ *Minibus*

Kleinwagen

German for Light Car.

→ *¹Voiturette*

Kleinstwagen

German for Microcar.

→ *Microcar*

Kocsi

Kocsi was an important carriage style invented circa 1460 in the Hungarian township of Kocs. It was of light construction and the bodywork was initially fixed unsuspended on two wheel axles. The excellence of the design lay in the use of choice wooden materials both for the body and the wheels, which made the vehicle flexible, light and strong and compensated for the lack of suspension. In consequence of this novel and later widely spread basic design the Hungarian name Kocsi (short for Kocsi szekér) went variously into other languages and eventually into German as Kutsche and English as Coach.

→ *¹Kutsche*

Kombi

A partly Continental European and Nordic term for Station Wagon *(q.v.)*. The word Kombi, used by itself, usually means the normal extended roof (Sedan-based) Station Wagon. A Kombi-coupé, on the other hand, is a short-roof three-door Hatchback, whereas a Kombi-sedan is its five-door equivalent.

Origins and history

The term Kombi originates from German Kombiwagen. Kombi, with the same signification, is in some languages spelled Combi. A modern higher and larger version of the Kombi or Station Wagon is the Minivan.

Kombiwagen ←

Kombi-coupé

Parts of northern European and Nordic countries use this term for a three-door Hatchback Coupe.
→ *Hatchback Coupe*
Kombi ←

Kombi-Limousine, dreitürig

German for a three-door Hatchback.
→ *Hatchback Coupé*
Kombi ←

Kombi-Limousine, fünftürig

German for a five-door Hatchback.
→ *Hatchback Sedan*
Kombi ←

Kombi-sedan

Parts of northern European and Nordic countries use this term for five-door Hatchback Sedan.
→ *Hatchback Sedan*
Kombi ←

Kombiwagen

German for Station Wagon (*q.v.*). The name derives from a vehicle that combines several uses—i.e., a Station Wagon type of vehicle, usually abbreviated Kombi.
Station Wagon ←

Kompakt

German for Compact.
→ *Compact*

Kupee

German (arch.) for Coupé. Original German spelling but rarely seen today, as the French Coupé seems to have taken over.
→ *Coupé*

Kupee-Kabriolett

German (arch.) for both a two to three seater Convertible Coupe and also a Cabriolet de Ville/Convertible Town Car.
→ *Cabriolet de Ville; Cabriolet 2/3 Plätze; Convertible Coupe*

[1]Kutsche

German for an early unsuspended horse-drawn Coach of various designs. Both the term Kutsche and its construction originated in the Hungarian township of Kocs (*see Kocsi*). The term Kutsche became also informally and generally used for any early open horse-drawn carriage for persons. (It has not been possible to study the track width relative to the carriage width, but it is assumed that the turning radius of these early vehicles must have been large.)
→ *[1]Carriage; [1]Coach*
Kocsi ←

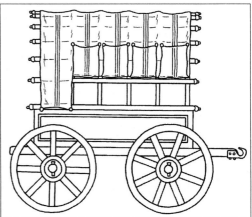

[1]Kutsche. An unsuspended German Kutsche for conveying persons, having a body as it could have looked in the mid–16th century (illustration based on illustrations appearing in Lásló Tarr's Karren Kutsche Karosse).

[2]Kutsche

German for a large four-wheeled enclosed horse-drawn carriage for several passengers with two doors, an elevated seat in front for the coachman and suspension by leather slings and or leaf springs.

→ *¹Coach*

³Kutsche

German, very informal, for a very old, large four-wheeled motor vehicle.

-L-

L

This is one of a few subtype designations that car manufacturers have consciously given a meaning. It has been employed to indicate "Leicht" (German for light), "Longue" (French for long), "Leggera" (Italian for light), "Lunga" (Italian for long), "Lusso" (Italian for luxury) and "Luxe" (luxury). One car manufacturer has conceded to the author that L, for luxury, merely indicated the lowest and most paltry degree of equipment and accessories in one of their Sedans.

Ladies Driving Phaeton

British alternative term for Park Phaeton.

→ *¹Duc*

¹Landau

A horse-drawn four-wheeled carriage

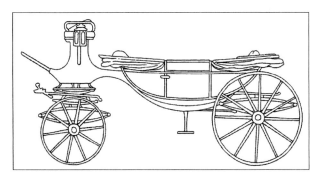

¹Landau. The Landau carriage led to the Landaulet automobile body style.

with a raised seat outside in front for the coachman and two passenger seat benches facing each other, usually for four passengers. For weather protection one forward and one backward folding hood could be pulled over the passenger compartment. The term originates from a carriage used in 1702 and 1704 by the Austrian Emperor Joseph I to travel from Vienna to inspect his troops which were besieging the German town of Landau in Pfalz, Bavaria. The interest shown locally in the Emperor's carriage subsequently resulted in production in Landau of carriages of similar style (Sallmann). These carriages became known as "Landauer," and this carriage style enjoyed its main popularity in the 19th century. The Landau can be compared to the Calèche and the Victoria carriages—however, both of these are lighter and have only one folding hood. The automobile derivation, Landaulet, stems from a small version of the Landau carriage.

Calèche ←
Language varieties
American: Landau.
British: Landau.
French: Landau.
German: Landauer.
Italian: Landò.
→ *²Landaulet*

²Landau

American alternative term for a Landaulet automobile *(see ²Landaulet)*. In the 1920s the term Landau was often combined with a bodywork style name (e.g., Landau Sedan), the Landau part deriving from dummy Landau bars *(q.v.)* in the rear body Quarters. From about 1930 and up to 1975 the vehicles did not sport Landau bars but the name stuck.

Landau bars

External, and sometimes internal, functional fitment to Convertible bodywork in order to prop up and guide the forward movement when unfolding a foldable top, and further to brace and maintain the top form when erect. In the past Landau bars were also used as external dummy decorations on non-foldable tops, one of the famous bodywork styles in this category being the Faux-cabriolet *(q.v.)*. Thus, Landau bars were also applied by some American auto manufacturers, mainly in the 1920s, to the rear Quarter panels of some Sedans in an effort to add visual attraction to the bodywork style. Some Kissel and Elcar automobiles managed to squeeze in oval Opera windows in front of dummy Landau bars in the rather limited space that normally constitutes the rear Quarters of a fairly average sized Sedan body style.

Language varieties

American: Landau bars.
British: Landau arms (colloquially also Pram irons).
French: Compas.
German: Sturmstangen.
Italian: Compasso.

Landauer

German for the horse-drawn Landau carriage.

➞ *Landau*

¹Landaulet

Landaulet was a small horse-drawn Landau carriage with only one (forward) folding top, otherwise having little in common with the Landau carriage proper. Landaulet is an internationally used term for this style of carriage. However, in German the correct spelling is Landaulett. The Landaulet name was eventually transferred to the automobile coachbuilding trade.

¹Landau ⬅

²Landaulet

An automobile with a folding roof behind the rear doors over the rearmost Quarter of the passenger compartment and having an open chauffeur's seat separated from the passenger compartment by a glass division. Normal passenger capacity was for three persons. Five passengers could be accommodated with foldable occasional seats. The Landaulet was a vehicle not immediately associated with out-of-town travel.

Origins and history

The Landaulet automobile inherited its rear Quarter folding roof characteristic direct from the horse-drawn Landaulet carriage.

¹Landaulet ⬅

Important period

First three decades of the 20th century. *See also Landaulet-Limousine.*

Variations

This type of car in a simpler form and generally with a passenger compartment for just three passengers became widely used in Europe as a taxi-cab during the second and third decades of the 20th century and was known in some countries as the Landaulet-Fiacre. Early Landaulets had no driver protection at all, but later, when the roof was lengthened forward to cover the driver's area, the

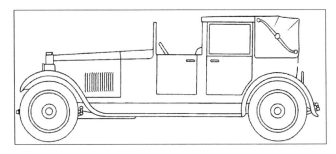

[2]Landaulet. The Landaulet had no weather protection for the chauffeur. The short passenger compartment, illustrated here, was referred to by the British as Single Landaulet (as opposed to the long Three-quarter Landaulet).

vehicle became larger and termed Landaulet-Limousine *(q.v.)*. In Great Britain, a Threequarter Landaulet had four side windows in the passenger compartment; a Single Landaulet had two. A Landaulet without a division would be referred to as a Saloon Landaulet.

Language varieties

Landaulet is the correct spelling (originally French). The designation Landaulet was applied more or less worldwide to this bodywork style. The carriage term Landau was sometimes used in America for Landaulet automobiles, as an alternative to the Landaulet name.

American: Landaulet, Landau.
British: Landaulet.
French: Landaulet.
German: Landaulett.
Italian: Landaulet.

→ *Landaulet-Fiacre; Landaulet-Limousine*

Landaulet de Ville

The Landaulet automobile was mainly used in cities and towns so "de Ville" in combination with Landaulet is essentially a pleonasm.

→ *Landaulet*

Landaulet-Fiacre

French for an early taxi (Fiacre) with foldable rear Quarter roof behind the passenger compartment doors, like the Landaulet. Renault produced the famous "Taxi de la Marne" of this description, the Renault type AG1, which transported thousands of soldiers to the east front to defend France during World War I.

→ *Taxi*
[2]*Fiacre;* [2]*Landaulet* ←

Landaulet-Limousine

An originally French bodywork term. The distinctive feature of this (usually coachbuilt) bodywork style, as compared to the normal Landaulet automobile, is the relative comfort of the chauffeur in front of the glass division. Thus, the Limousine designation indicates that the front driver area is at least windshielded and roofed. Three to five passengers could ride in the rear compartment. As in the Landaulet, the rearmost passengers had the option of

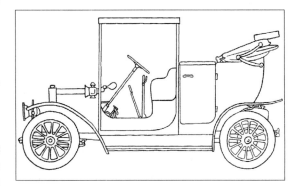

Landaulet-Limousine. The distinguishing feature, as compared to the Landaulet, is the roofed chauffeur's compartment.

enjoying fresh air by opening the collapsible rear Quarter hood. This, of course, confirms the body style as a Landaulet.

Origins and history

Like the coachman of the horse-drawn Landau carriage, the chauffeur of the original Landaulet car was sitting entirely in the open. The "Limousine" distinction came with the roof over the driver's compartment, around 1910.

²Landaulet ←

Important period

Ca. 1910 to mid–1930s.

Variations

Like the Landaulet-Fiacre, this Landaulet-Limousine body style came to be utilized as a Taxi. The chauffeur's roof provided a place to fit roof racks for customers' luggage. A Landaulet-Limousine style of bodywork where the division glass had been omitted was in Great Britain referred to as a Saloon Landaulet.

Language varieties

American: Limousine Landaulet.

British: Limousine Landaulet.

French: Landaulet-Limousine.

German: Landaulett-Limousine.
Italian: Landaulet-Limousine.
→ *²Limousine*

Landaulette

Variant and futile spelling of Landaulet (not used in French speaking countries). Though the term would imply a *small* Landaulet, vehicles so named rarely were.

²Landaulet ←

Leichenwagen

German for Hearse.
→ *Hearse*

Lift-back, Liftback

An early British variety for Hatchback. Liftback is also an alternative (colloquial) German term for a three- or five-door Hatchback vehicle.
→ *¹Hatchback*

Light Car

A proper small car with open or enclosed bodywork in Convertible, Coupe and Sedan form. After World War I the Light Car became established, primarily in Europe, as a reliable small automobile having a small four cylinder engine (as opposed to the singles or twins of the usually open Cyclecars and Tri-

Light Car. A British open Light Car from the post–World War I period.

cars) and propeller shaft rear-wheel drive. English for Voiturette.
→ *¹Voiturette*

Limo

²Limousine ←
American abbreviation for Limousine.

¹Limousine/Limo

A chauffeur-driven automobile having an elaborately appointed rear pas-

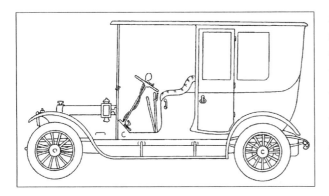

¹Limousine. The earliest Limousine had only a (fixed) roof for chauffeur weather protection.

senger compartment separated from the chauffeur by a glass division or partition. For protection, the chauffeur originally had only a windshield and a permanent roof, but later low windowless doors were added to the driving compartment. Three to five passengers could be seated in the enclosed rear compartment; other Limousines had a somewhat larger five-passenger compartment with occasional seats and usually four side windows. The bodywork of this type of automobile was mostly coachbuilt.

Origins and history

Limousine is the feminine form of the French region of Limousin. There are two theories about the origins of Limousine as a vehicle body style designation: Either the protective wide cloak or mantle used by goods carriage personnel in Limousin, France, or the woollen cloth coverage made in Limousin to protect goods loaded in open wagons from inclement weather. Apparently Limousine was never applied to a horse-drawn vehicle. A group of open-fronted chauffeur-driven cars in the period between the two World Wars were generally used for mainly city/town commuting and short journeys. When country

roads improved, possibilities arose for traveling longer distances by car and it became obvious with longer journeys and higher speeds that the driver needed more weather protection. When the early Berline, Coupé de Ville and Brougham automobiles were furnished with a fixed roof for the chauffeur these body styles became effectively Limousines. Up to World War I the Limousine style bodywork appears to have been almost the only completely enclosed automobile body style. The origins of the term suggest that it could be correct to apply the term Limousine to any enclosed motor vehicle—this is indeed borne out by British descriptions of the two-seater "Coupé Limousine" car and a "Saloon Limousine" (Shepherd, 1923), in addition to the fact that in Germany the term Limousine is being used almost indiscriminately, both in combination and individually, to denote any enclosed passenger vehicle (except a multi-passenger bus). Thus, even enclosed single-seater racing cars have in German been termed "Renn-Limousine." However, in other languages than German the original meaning of shelter/enclosure seems largely to have become lost; thus fairly contradictory terms for non-enclosed vehicles are being used, e.g. Convertible Stretchlimo.

Coupé de Ville ←
Important period

From the first decade of the 20th century up to the early 1920s.

²Limousine/Limo

A large, long wheelbase, completely

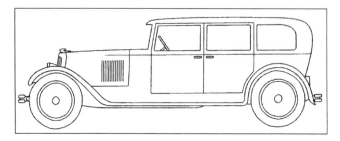

²Limousine. In the decades prior to World War II the Limousine became fully enclosed.

enclosed chauffeur-driven automobile with the chauffeur separated from the large, usually luxurious passenger compartment, or "saloon," by a glass division which was, in its most formal form, permanently fixed. Normally occasional seats are provided for additional passengers. Limousines are generally four-door, six-windowed cars seating seven to nine passengers. The rearmost side (Quarter) windows are usually quite large ones. To be quite strict, the term Limousine should only be applied to large cars with a division between the chauffeur and the passenger compartment.

¹*Limousine* ←

Important period

Early 1920s to present.

Variations

A Limousine with facilities for carrying luggage for long-distance travel was sometimes referred to as a Touring Limousine. In some countries "Limousine" is applied to large vehicles for more than six passengers which are not necessarily chauffeur driven and, therefore, sometimes have no division. In Italy the chauffeur of a Limousine is consistently separated by a glass division, and if the chauffeur's compartment is completely enclosed the full term is Limousine Guida interna *(q.v.);* otherwise Limousine. A very long and later period Limousine is the Stretch-limo.

Language varieties

Whereas the original Limousine meaning of shelter, (referring to the chauffeur's being permanently protected), seems to have been fairly consistently sustained in Germany, this has not been the case in many other countries, including the Anglo-American ones, where it appears that Limousine in many cases has taken on the meaning of large passenger vehicle irrespective of whether the chauffeur has weather protection or not. Therefore, the English designation "enclosed Limousine" or "enclosed drive Limousine" is known to have been used to specify a fully enclosed vehicle. A rather surprising term, though somewhat rare to-day, is the Convertible Stretch-limo for a completely open very large car. Today Limousine is an international term, generally understood to mean a large, chauffeur-driven, enclosed six-windowed automobile with division and passenger compartment for at least six persons.

American: Limousine/Limo.

British: Limousine, Pullman Limousine.

French: Chauffeur-limousine.

German: Pullman-Limousine.

Italian: Limousine Guida interna.

Limousine, 4 Sitze

German for Close-coupled Sedan.

→ *Berlinetta; Close-coupled*

Limousine allungata

Italian for a Stretch-limo with division.

→ *Stretch-limo*

Limousine Brougham

American for a Limousine Town Car, a large five to seven passenger Brougham which exhibits the typical Brougham body style features *(see ²Brougham)*. A Limousine Brougham having windows in the rear Quarters could be specified as a Glass quarter Brougham. With the rear Quarters paneled the full designation would be Panel Brougham. The Limousine prefix has not been consistently used to specify a large Brougham.

→ *Limousine Town Car*
²Brougham ←

Limousine de Ville

British for Limousine Town Car. This term was particularly favored by British coachbuilders for large Coupé de Ville–style bodywork in the period between the World Wars, the capacious passenger compartment having four windows, or sometimes two windows and paneled rear Quarters. Like the name Limousine Town Car, the term is inherently flawed, as the significance of "Limousine" is "cover" or "shelter" whereas the chauffeur of early examples was subject to the elements without even a simple canopy. An almost alternative term for this style of bodywork is Sedanca *(q.v.)*.

→ *Limousine Town Car*

Limousine Guida interna

Italian for a chauffeur driven large car with the enclosed chauffeur's compartment separated from the passenger compartment by a glass division.

Variations
A smaller chauffeur driven car is the Berlina Guida interna.

→ *Berlina Guida interna; ²Limousine*

Limousine Landaulet

American and British alternative for Landaulet-Limousine.

→ *Landaulet-Limousine*

Limousine Town Car

The Limousine Town Car was a large variation of the normal Town Car having an enclosed luxurious compartment with usually four side windows and seating capacity in the passenger compartment for five to seven people. The chauffeur sat in the open. In later models the chauffeur's compartment was usually provided with doors and a folding canopy for weather protection. There was always a division glass. The bodywork of these cars was normally built by coachbuilders. For illustration, *see Coupé Limousine.*

Origins and history
"Limousine" meant originally "covered" or "sheltered." *(See ¹Limousine.)* In the first half of the 20th century the name became gradually used to denote simply "large car," which accounts for its somewhat dubious use for an early Town Car with the chauffeur sitting in the open. However, when the driver's compartment became fully enclosed the car became in effect a Limousine in the original sense of the term *(see ²Limousine)*.

Town Car ←

Important period
1920s up to World War II.

Variations
Instead of having four rear side windows, the rearmost large Quarters were sometimes paneled and only the passenger compartment doors had windows. This body style was sometimes termed Panel Limousine Town Car.

Language varieties
The Limousine prefix was not always

used to specify the size of a large Town Car. In America a Limousine Town Car having the Brougham styling characteristics was also known as Limousine Brougham.

American: Limousine Town Car.
British: Limousine de Ville, Sedanca.
French: Coupé Limousine.
German: Stadt-Limousine, 4-fenstrig.
Italian: Coupé Limousine, Coupé di Citta, 4 vetri.

Limousine, Vier Sitze

German for Close-coupled Sedan.
➼ *Berlinetta; Close-coupled*

Low-chassis

A low-built chassis results usually in a low body style, which has led to the use of this term, in normal parlance, to describe a low-built bodywork. With cars using rigid wheel axles of the pre-unitary chassis construction period, one efficient method of achieving a low build was to locate the axles—usually the rear one, sometimes both front and rear—and suspension members above the chassis frame members. For illustration, *see Underslung*.

Language varieties
American: Low-chassis, Underslung.
British: Low-chassis, Underslung.
French: Surbaissé.
German: Tiefergelegt.
Italian: Ribassato.
➼ *Surbaissé; Underslung*

-M-

M

Car subtype designation used by some British, French and German marquees. The M designation of BMW, derived from their Motorsport division, has become a characteristic type prefix, applied initially to BMW racing cars and subsequently to quite a few of their sporting Sedans, Sports Cars and Sports Coupés. The significance of M is not dissimilar to that of Ti.
➼ *Ti*

Macchina

Italian colloquial term for car. Alternative to Auto.
➼ *⁶Car*

Macchina da corsa

Italian for Racing Car.
➼ *Racing Car*

Mehrzweck-Fahrzeug

German formal and technical term for Minivan and Compact minivan.
➼ *[1,2]Minivan; MPW*

Microbus

Microbus is a term used in North America for essentially a Minibus *(q.v.)*.

Microcar

Term used to describe a very small car having bodywork to hold just two persons and not very much else. Some very small European cars built just after World War II were Three-wheelers. The term Microcar may carry different values between the United States and the rest of the world. Thus, an American Microcar could be seen in Europe as a larger small vehicle than "micro," whereas a European Microcar could be

Microcar. The need for a small car has always existed. Scarcity of materials and fuel immediately after World War II resulted in production of very small cars.

considered ridiculously small in the United States. (A somewhat larger car than a Microcar is in this work termed Minicar.)

Important period
Mid–1940s to present.
Language varieties
American: Microcar or Micro City-car.
British: Microcar.
French: Citadine.
German: Kleinstwagen.
Italian: Microvettura.
→ *Bubblecar; Tricar*

Microvettura

Italian for Microcar *(q.v.)*.

Mid-van, Midivan

Continental European colloquial and loosely used terms for Minivan. Since Minivan and MPV have gained wide acceptance these terms have largely fallen out of use.
→ *Minivan*

¹Milord

A Victoria style of horse-drawn coachman-driven carriage having a Victoria folding hood and usually a rear Spider (Rumble) seat. The Milord and

Victoria carriages were in principle similar with the exception of the Spider seat. The English name Mylord was applied in France as Milord to this style of carriage. The use and spelling of this term in Continental Europe was inconsistent.
¹Landau ←
Variations
An almost similar style of carriage with a shorter wheelbase and mostly with a rear Spider seat was usually known as Spider outside English speaking areas.
→ *¹Spider; ¹Victoria*

²Milord

An early automobile with a Victoria style hood for the passengers. Sometimes spelled Mylord.

³Milord

This term, and Coupé Milord, has sometimes been applied to two-door Cabriolet cars with a semi-foldable top.
→ *Cabriolet-victoria*

Minibus

The Minibus style of multi-passenger bodywork is perhaps more typical for Europe and Far East than North America. The bodywork is like a miniature bus usually built on a Platform slightly larger than that of a normal European-sized car.
Origins and history
In Europe the pervasive first Minibus was manufactured by Volkswagen in the 1950s and given the incontrovertible type name "Bus." The idea to build such a vehicle is reputed to have origi-

nated with a Dutch-
man of the Dutch
VW importer, who
presented the Volks-
wagen factory with a
sketch showing the
general concept based
on the ubiquitous
rear-engined   VW
Beetle.

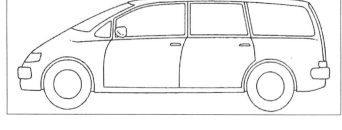

Minivan. The "mini" part of the term seems somewhat out of place, as this style of vehicle is mostly a quite large automobile.

Important period
1950s to present.
Variations
A vehicle for the same purpose but with a greater passenger capacity is the Passenger Van.
Language varieties
Minibus is an informal and colloquial name in some countries outside the United States for Passenger Van *(q.v.)*.
American: Microbus.
British: Minibus.
French: Petit Bus.
German: Kleinbus.
Italian: Minibus.

Minicar

Contemporary term for a small car that is a little larger than a Microcar. The bodywork of a Minicar usually has seating capacity for four persons. Alternative term: Compact. (The prefix "Mini" is a relative entity—compare e.g. Minivan.)
→ *Microcar*

Mini People-carrier

British for a Compact minivan.
→ *²Minivan*

¹Minivan

A large and high roofed, usually front-wheel drive, Station Wagon (or small Passenger Van) type of vehicle having a seating capacity sometimes for

as many as eight. A characteristic of the Minivan body style is its lack of Boxes, or separate body structures for engine and luggage compartment *(see Box)*.
Origins and history
In America in the fall of 1983 Chrysler's Plymouth Voyager and Dodge Caravan initiated the Minivan vogue, closely followed in Europe in 1984 by the Renault Espace. A variety of sizes of vehicles with this kind of bodywork have since been produced by a large number of manufacturers, all having the characteristic of increased height compared to the Station Wagon/Estate Car/Kombi, giving great capacity for seating or luggage, or both. In the United States USA the Minivan and the SUV *(q.v.)* have largely superseded the Station Wagon.
Passenger Van; Station Wagon ←
Important period
1980s to present.
Variations
A more utilitarian style of vehicle for roughly the same purpose is the Minibus.
Language varieties
MPV derives from Multi-purpose Vehicle.
American: Minivan.
British: MPV, People-carrier.
French: Monospace, Monovolume, Monocorps.

German (formal and technical): Mehrzweck-Fahrzeug.

German (general): MPW, Minivan.

Italian: Monovolume, Multispazio, Minivan.

[2]Minivan

A Compact minivan—in effect a mix between a full-size MPV and a very small Station Wagon. The bodywork is usually based on the Platform of a small Saloon/Sedan, but is short and high. Seating capacity is up to six. For illustration, *see Compact minivan*.

Language varieties

American: Compact minivan.

British: Mini People-carrier, MPC.

French: Monocorps, Monovolume.

German (formal and technical): Mehrzweck-Fahrzeug.

German (general): MPW, Minivan.

Italian: Monovolume.

Monocoque

French for unitary construction. An alternative term is Carrosserie autoporteuse.

→ *Unitary construction*

Monocorps

French for Minivan and Compact minivan.

→ [1,2]*Minivan*

Monoposto

Literally "single-seater" in Italian. Well-known term also outside Italy to differentiate from two-seater racing cars.

→ *Racing Car*

Monoscocca

Italian for unitary construction (Monocoque).

→ *Unitary construction*

Monospace

French for Minivan. Alternatives: Monovolume, Monocorps.

→ [1,2]*Minivan*

Monovolume

Italian and French for Minivan and Compact minivan.

→ [1,2]*Minivan*

Motor

Motor was a British colloquial abbreviation for Motor Car, used mainly into the 1920s, subsequently to become just Car.

→ [6]*Car*

Motor Buggy

An American very early, light, open two-seater motor propelled vehicle on high and slim wheels, rather similar to its horse-drawn Buggy counterpart. For weather protection usually only a Victoria-type folding top. *See also Highwheeler.*

[1]*Buggy* ←

[1]Motor Car, Motorcar

A more formal term for Car in English.

→ [6]*Car*

[2]Motor Car, Motorcar

A railway car, either self-propelled electric (British) or with various means of propulsion (American).

Motor Tricycle

→ *Tricycle*

MPC

British short for Mini People-carrier; i.e., a Compact minivan.

→ [2]*Minivan*

MPV

Abbreviation for Multi Purpose Vehicle. MPV could infer a number of vehicles having multiple purposes but in Europe these initials are understood as Minivan.

→ *Minivan*

MPW

German alternative for the Minivan and Compact minivan. MPW is an abbreviation for Mehr Personen Wagen ("More passengers vehicle").

→ [1, 2] *Minivan*

Multi Purpose Vehicle

Full name for MPV.

→ *Minivan*

Multispazio

Italian alternative for Monovolume.

→ [1] *Minivan*

Muscle Car

An American term originating in the 1960s with the Pontiac Tempest Le Mans GTO; a high-powered mid-sized two-door car in Hardtop and Convertible forms to compete in the Ponycar sector of the market. Other car makers subsequently produced cars for this category.

→ *Ponycar*

Mylord

Original English spelling of Milord. Used in Continental Europe alternatively for Milord.

→ *Milord*

-N-

Notchback

A (usually Sedan) body having a more or less distinct notch behind the rear window. In the modern car this notch

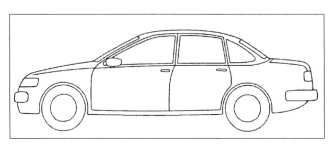

Notchback. A European Notch- or Bustleback Sedan style car.

is becoming ever less accentuated. A car with a less pronounced notch behind the rear window is sometimes referred to as a "Semi Fastback." The term

Notchback is used particularly to distinguish a car body style from a Fastback one. "Three-box" (as opposed to Two-box/Fastback) is an alternative, technically oriented, term.

Language varieties

American: Notchback, Three-box or (colloquial) Bustleback.

British: Three-box or Notch-back.

French: Carrosserie trois volumes.

German: Stufenheck or Drei-Zellenstruktur.

Italian: Tre volumi, Three-box or Notchback.

-O-

Occasional four

British alternative to Chummy *(q.v.)*.

Off-roader

Generic for, normally, a four-wheel drive (4x4) car. The practical body-works of many modern off-road or cross-country vehicles, typically with external spare wheel, reflect their utilitarian, and sometimes recreational, purpose besides their capacity for transporting people. Three or five doors. The rear door may be side hinged, transversely hinged at the upper edge (Lift-back) or a split combination of the two. Off-roader vehicles exist to-day in all permutations from the most spartan to the most luxurious.

Origins and history

Off-road vehicles have been made since the first World War, initially for military purposes only. In between the World Wars many designs emerged, the American Jeep *(q.v.)* constituting the classic open top World War II scout and passenger vehicle.

Important period

1914 to present.

Variations

The variations on the Off-roader theme are too numerous to list. As an example, the SUV is a modern and quite comfortable Off-roader (although in actual practice not very much used off road) originally based on the conventional Station Wagon. The Beach Buggy is a two- or four-wheel driven off-road vehicle. However, lest anyone think all Off-roaders must be four-wheel drive, note that 6x6 (six-wheel drive) open (Cabriolet) six to seven seater military staff cars (with two rear wheel axles) were manufactured by e.g. Daimler-Benz in the late 1930s and by Krupp in the early 1940s.

Berliet in France produced in 1927 an open six-wheeled military vehicle with one central wheel axle and four-wheel steering and drive via the front and rear axles. There were numerous others.

Language varieties

American: Off-roader.
British: Off-roader.
French: Tout-terrains.
German: Geländewagen.
Italian: Fuoristrada.
→ *Four-by-four (4x4); Jeep; SUV*

Open Car

A generic phrase for any car configured (or configurable) for open-air travel. In England, in the early 1930s, an open car was described in *The Motoring Encyclopedia* as follows:

"The open car has shown a steady decline in popularity and the closed a steady increase. This change over has been largely contributed to by the success of the sunshine roofs and the improved ventilation and window arrangements in the closed cars of recent manufacture. The open car, however, shows no sign of dying out altogether, for it still finds favor in all sports types."

Language varieties

"Open," loosely and without defining type of bodywork, can be expressed in

French as Cabriolet, in German as Cabrio and in Italian as Aperto.

→ *Cabriolet*

Opera, Opéra

A term applied by some coach-builders to luxurious vehicles to denote the facility to carry extra passengers by e.g. occasional collapsible seating. In the period ca. 1915 to 1980 extra, usually oval, rear Quarter windows both on four-door Sedan as well as Coupe body-work used to be called Opera windows. Coupe cars of the later period some-times sported forward leaning rectangular rear Quarter Opera windows.

Opera Coupe

→ *Coupé Opéra*

Owner-driver

American and British for a non-chauffeur-driven automobile. In America the Owner-driver term seems to have been seldom used. Terms in German and Italian meaning precisely Owner-driver seem to be lacking. For French, *see Conduite Intérieure.*

-P-

P

An Italian subtype designation; abbreviation for Posteriore, meaning "rear" and used for mid-engined Sports Cars.

Panel Brougham

A Brougham having the rear Quarters paneled instead of windowed. The opposite style is the Glass quarter Brougham.

→ *Limousine Brougham*

Panneau AR fuyant

French alternative to Carrosserie deux volumes for Fastback.

→ *Fastback*

Park Phaeton

British term for a Duc carriage.

→ *[1]Duc*

Parkwagen

German for a Duc style horse-drawn carriage.

→ *[1]Duc*

[1]Parlor Coach

An American term, essentially to describe a railroad carriage with a large undivided interior.

[2]Parlor Coach

A comfortable American enclosed, multi-passenger vehicle with usually rather bus-like bodywork, in the period approximately between the two World Wars, for touring and sight-seeing. As employed for general passenger conveyance by hotels and airline companies the Parlor Coach was largely superseded by the Stretch-limo and in many countries, later still, by the Passenger Van.

→ *Passenger Van; Stretch-limo*

Passenger Van

An enclosed goods van type of vehicle suitably fitted out with several side windows and multiple seating for up to ten or even fifteen passengers to meet

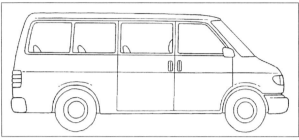

Passenger Van. A utilitarian alternative to the Stretch-limo.

demand from airline companies and hotels for a practical and more utilitarian alternative to the Stretch-limo.

Origins and history

Originally conceived as a smaller, enclosed commercial vehicle for goods transportation. Whereas the big American auto companies produce van-like vehicles specifically for passenger transportation, the tendency in Europe has been to adapt regular goods vans to accommodate people, and in recent years even to series produce them.

Stretch-limo ←

Important period

1970s to present.

Variations

The diverse national variations are innumerable, all adapted to local needs.

Language varieties

In some countries terms like Minibus are employed for this kind of passenger transportation vehicle.

American: Van.
British: Minibus, Van.
French: Petit bus, Van.
German: Kleinbus, Van.
Italian: Minibus, Van.

People Carrier

British alternative term for a large Minivan.

→ *¹Minivan*

Persenning

German for Tonneau-cover.

→ *⁴Tonneau*

Personenkraftwagen

German for automobile. Common abbreviation: PKW or Pkw.

→ *⁶Car*

Petit Bus

French for Minibus *(q.v.)*.

Petit Duc

An open, light and rather primitive two-seater motorized vehicle having simple bodywork, no doors but sometimes a folding top for weather protection. Sometimes also provided with a Rumble seat. The size of the Petit Duc is in the Voiturette (Light Car) category.

Origins and history

Although Duc means Duke in French, Petit Duc translates as "small owl." The Petit Duc was a lighter version of the Duc automobile. After 1905 the Petit Duc developed into the Phaéton. The Petit Duc was a typically French kind of vehicle.

Petit Duc. This was a French small automobile, in fact a Voiturette, from ca. 1904.

²Duc ←
Important period
1895–1905.
Variations
In normal French parlance such a vehicle is usually referred to as Duc, which really defines a slightly larger variation of the Petit Duc.
→ *²Phaeton*

Phaëthon

From Greek mythology; Phaëthon was the son of Olympian God Helios and his mistress Clymene. He drove his father's chariot (the Sun) through the sky but lost control and would have burned up the Earth had not Zeus struck him dead by a thunderbolt.
→ *Phaeton*

¹Phaeton

A four-wheeled open horse-drawn owner-driver carriage made in many forms in various parts of the world. Whereas the American Phaeton has been described as having a fairly straightforward body with a simple coachman's seat in front of a passengers' bench for two, some of the French Phaetons were richly decorated open four-seater carriages. On the other hand many of the British carriages were sporting so-called highflyer or perch-high owner-driver vehicles, often driven fast by the dashing young gentlemen of the time. The driver's seat of the British vehicles was always the more comfortable. In mid–19th century England the Ladies' Driving Phaeton emerged for, as stated by Parry, a "lady of quality to drive herself," the groom seated behind on a simpler Spider seat, or following on horseback. Typical for the later types of Phaeton carriages was their fairly light construction, which be-

came possible as road quality improved. For illustration , *see Spider 1.* As can be seen, one name was given to a number of quite dissimilar four-wheeled carriages—an unfortunate custom carried over to 20th century automobile coach-building and series production.
Origins and history
After having been established in antique mythology the name Phaéton appears to have become a denomination for the driver of an early farming cart. Thereafter a transition took place and Phaeton was applied to open horse-drawn carriages, according to Sallmann, in England in the first half of the 18th century. Around 1780 the name appeared in France applied to light two-wheeled, two-seater carriages (Garnier). Later in France, a four-wheeled light carriage almost comparable to the Phaeton was the Duc.
¹Duc; Phaëthon ←
Important period
Mid-eighteenth century to the beginning of the twentieth century.
Variations
A variation of the Phaeton carriage with connotations to the early automobile was the Spider (*see ¹,²Spider*).

²Phaeton

A primarily European open, light two to three seater automobile, initially without windshield and doors. For weather protection a simple foldable Victoria-type top was usually provided. Some very early specimens (as illustrated) followed one of the British carriage styles with the driver's perch far forward, an under-body engine and a single passenger's (footman's) rear seat. Later, about 1905, the engine moved forward and a bench seat for two and improved weather protection were pro-

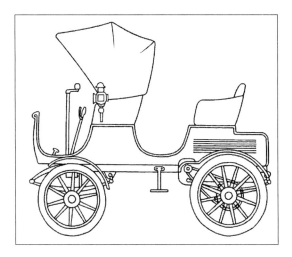

²Phaeton. A variation of the very early Phaeton with scarcely any bodywork at all and a rear under-body engine.

vided. In the United States only a few early two person vehicles were designated Phaeton (though some of them could equally well have been termed Runabouts), soon to be superseded by the Roadster (²*Roadster*).

Origins and history

While inheriting the name Phaeton from the horse-drawn carriage, in France the two-seater Phaéton was essentially an improvement after 1904 of the Petit Duc and the Duc *(q.v.)*.

²Petit Duc, ¹*Phaeton* ←

Important period
USA: 1900–1905.
Europe: 1900–1915.

Language varieties

The American use of this term for a two to three seater car was rare and inconsistent. In Europe, though originally and strictly a two-seater, the term Phaeton was later applied loosely to much larger vehicles *(see* ³*Phaeton, below)*.

American: Phaeton.
British: Tourer, Phaeton.
French: Phaéton.

German: Phaeton, Phaëton.
Italian: Phaéton.

³Phaeton

An open, rather sporty Touring automobile usually having comfortable seating for five, plus sometimes two foldable occasional seats. A simple, fully extendible and foldable top and usually detachable peg-on side curtains were provided. In the United States two distinct variations of Phaetons were produced; the *standard production* Phaeton, which a few manufacturers treated as identical to the Touring Car and therefore so named it, and the high-class, somewhat later and mostly *coachbuilt* Dual-cowl Phaeton which had a secondary cowl and windshield for the rear seat passengers. The latter is dealt with under its own heading. In Continental Europe the Double Phacton, or Phaeton, as it was normally called, was a much favored bodywork style up to the mid-twenties. Typically, the front and rear seats of the early European variation were of identical and rather plushy design. Moreover, early cars had only a simple foldable top for weather protection and no doors but in about 1910 rear doors started to appear and later a windscreen and canvas peg-on side curtains. By World War I the vehicle had acquired all the fully-fledged characteristics of the Double Phaeton, including the Torpedo-style cowl, or scuttle, between engine room and windshield and a more or less straight waist- or beltline. *See also Dual-cowl Phaeton, Double Phaeton, Torpedo*.

Origins and history

The origins of the name go back to antique times. As regards the automotive body style, the ancestry can be traced to the open Tonneau bodywork from the turn of the 20th century. It would appear that in America the Phaeton name was applied by manufacturers to some fairly normal Touring Cars, likely in order to enhance their attractiveness. Later, in the mid–1920s such cars were complemented by the high-class, usually coachbuilt, Dual-cowl Phaeton body style. In Europe, typical of the early Double Phaeton automobiles were the comfortable semi-baroque style seat design inherited from the Tonneau. The Double Phaeton body style was more or less superseded in France and Italy by the three- or four-door Torpédo coachwork when the design of the seating became integrated with the bodywork. Also the body acquired a continuous, or almost continuous, line from the top of the bonnet sides rearwards along the body waistline. Manufacturers were less than consistent in their use of the name Phaeton on early vehicles—a tradition inherited from the horse-drawn carriage age.

Phaëthon; Tonneau ←
Important period
USA: 1910–1935.
Europe: 1906–1930.
Variations
Although the second windshield on a cowl behind the front seats was archetypal of the American coachbuilt (Dual-cowl) Phaeton, this variation did also find favor with some European coachbuilders on expensive chassis in the 1920s. Instead of the fully extensible folding top, a few early specimens were built with a short Victoria top just over the rear seat. Another early and rare variation was the fixed roof secured to the windshield at the front and about

six side and hind pillars, being otherwise completely open to the sides. After World War II the name Phaeton was applied by quite a few American auto manufacturers rather haphazardly to some (single cowl) two- and four-door open vehicles, probably in an effort to improve their images. In 2002 Volkswagen introduced a large Sedan under the model name Phaeton, though it bears no resemblance to the Phaeton body style.

(Note: Phaeton strictly speaking is a two-seater; a Double or Dual-cowl Phaeton seats four to seven passengers; a Triple Phaeton has three rows of transverse seats and holds up to nine passengers.)

Language varieties
Phaeton, Torpedo and the European equivalents of Touring Car are known to have been used indiscriminately in Europe for roughly similarly bodied automobiles.

American: Phaeton, Dual-cowl Phaeton.
British: Tourer, Phaeton.
French: Phaéton, Double Phaéton.
German: Phaeton, Phaëton, Doppelphaeton.
Italian: Phaéton, Doppio Phaéton.
→ *Double Phaeton; Triple Phaeton*

PKW, Pkw

German short for Personenkraftwagen.
→ *⁶Car*

Plate-forme

French for Platform.
→ *Platform*

Platform

Platform is an American contemporary term for the horizontal steel construction which forms the basis for attaching the engine, drive line, suspension, steering, bodywork etc. from which the modern car is built up integrally into one unit.

American: Platform.
British: Floorpan.
French: Plate-forme.
→ *Unitary construction*

Pointe Bateau

French for Boattail.
→ *Boattail*

Pointe Bordino

French for a Bordino style tail.
→ *Bordino*

Ponton

A French and German term to describe slab-sided car bodywork, deriving, of course, from the pontoon form. "Barchetta" in Italian expresses the same slab-sidedness, but this term applies specifically to an open sporting car. For illustration—*see Barchetta*.

Italian: Ponton-side.

Ponycar

An American term derived from the equine name of the Ford Mustang, the car which defined the type. A strictly four-seater car, in either Convertible or Hardtop form, with sporty aspirations.

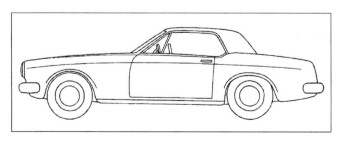

Ponycar. **The Ponycar has an individual style and a sporty disposition without actually being a Sports Car.**

Origins and history

Late 1950s marketing investigations by Ford of USA revealed that a car with sporting traits aimed at the young people would be a viable proposition. In fact, the subsequently produced vehicle appealed to a lot of not-so-young people as well. A long hood and cabin set well back on the chassis gave the original Mustang character, and the press and public gave this type of vehicle the Ponycar epithet. The Ford Mustang led to a great following and competition from other makers.

Important period
1964–1973.

Variations

The first, and "real," Ford Mustang was produced—with significant changes over the years to bodywork, chassis and engine—until 1973. The next variation was much smaller, consistent with increasing world oil and fuel prices at the time. Other car producers tried to emulate the original Mustang concept with varying success.

→ *Muscle Car*

Porte-Chaise

French for Sedan Chair.
→ *²Sedan*

Prachtwagen

German for Gala or State Coach. Alternative to Galawagen.

Carrozza ←

Professional Car

American synonym for Hearse.
→Hearse

Profilé

A French term to describe streamlining or a streamlined bodywork.

American: Stream-
line.
   British: Streamline.
   French: Profilé.
   German: Stromlin-
ienform.
   Italian: Aerodinam-
ica.

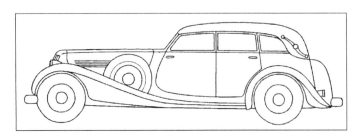

Pullman-Kabriolett. This is a typically German pre–World War II Convertible Limo.

Promiscuo

Italian alternative
for Station Wagon. The Promiscuo is
suitable for transporting both passengers and cargo. Seldom more than three
doors.
   → *Familiare*

Pukka

Anglo-Indian term for genuine or
perfectly constructed. In this work
Pukka is used particularly to emphasize
genuineness in a Sports Car *(q.v.)*.

¹Pullman

A luxurious railroad coach; also called
Pullman car, or a railroad sleeping-car.

²Pullman

Pullman has been used variously in
diverse languages to denote a luxurious
and large passenger vehicle. It has also
been applied as a complementary German term in combination with other
bodywork terms to describe a long
motor vehicle. The term is often, but
not exclusively, associated with Mercedes-Benz cars.
   → *Pullman-Kabriolett; Pullman-
Limousine*

Pullman-Cabriolet

German alternative spelling of Pullman-Kabriolett *(q.v.)*.

Pullman-Kabriolett

German term for a long open, comfortable, sometimes chauffeur-driven,
Convertible vehicle for more than five
or six passengers. Pullman-Kabriolett is
also applicable to a stretched open vehicle for seven to nine passengers *(see
also Convertible Stretch Limo)*.
   Language varieties
   American: Convertible Limo.
   British: 4-door Drop-head Limousine with occasional seats.
   French: Cabriolet/Décapotable à 6–7
places.
   German: Pullman-Kabriolett, Pullman-Cabriolet.
   Italian: Cabriolet a 6–7 posti.
   → *³Cabriolet*

Pullman-Limousine

German term for a long enclosed,
comfortable, sometimes chauffeur-driven, Limousine for more than five or six
passengers.
   → *Stretch Limo*

-Q-

Quadriciclo

Italian for Quadricycle. There are a couple of current Italian Quadriciclo vehicle types which are light and low-powered. The driver of one of them is required to have only a motorcycle driver's license.

→ *Quadricycle*

Quadricycle

Early four-wheeled light open self-propelled vehicle with very rudimentary bodywork and light wire-spoked wheels shod with solid rubber tires.

[1]Quarter

Originally the rear corners in the passenger compartment of an automobile—*see Single* and *Three-quarter.*

[2]Quarter

In the period before and after World

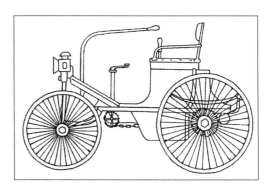

Quadricycle. The European Quadricycle could in some respects be compared with the American Stanhope automobile.

War II, before the advent of air-conditioning systems, the small swiveling ventilation windows in the front part of the front doors were called Quarter windows.

-R-

Race Car, Racing Car

A single-seater ("monoposto") car for racing competition, with as simple and light bodywork as possible. No form of road equipment. The road wheels are almost always without fenders (hence the term "open wheelers"). The illustration shows a modern Formula 1 car with wings and airdams to improve road wheel adhesion. The exterior bodywork is normally cluttered with advertising.

> ***Language varieties***
> *American*: Race Car.
> *British*: Racing Car.
> *French*: Voiture de course.
> *German*: Rennwagen.
> *Italian*: Vettura da corsa, Macchina da corsa.

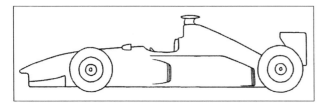

Race Car. The single-seater track Racing Car represents the fastest race category, with bodywork designed to add traction to the road wheels.

Racing Coupés and Sedans

For racing purposes Coupé and Sedan cars, with their external bodywork basically in their original forms but sometimes augmented with airdams, foils, fenders etc., are categorized in various racing classes and formulæ under a number of names. Modifications to engine and chassis are usually allowed. It is difficult to see the logic behind the naming of such race categories as the Touring Car Championship, for touring leisurely around is certainly not what these race vehicles are doing

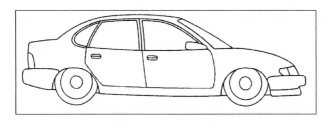

Racing Sedan. The usually much modified Racing Sedan cannot (and should not) carry passengers.

Racing Sports Car/Race Sports Car

A two-seater regulation bodied Sports Car produced or modified for racing and therefore made utterly simple, with spartan bodywork. Earlier cars had road wheel fenders; modern cars have all-enveloping bodywork. Some specialized Racing Sports Car formulæ allow bodywork styles that are only in principle two-seaters. These cars are usually not road registered.

Language varieties
American: Race Sports Car

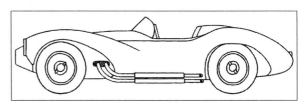

Racing Sports Car. A road registered Sports Car for racing has very spartan bodywork and represents the fastest of all road registered vehicles.

British: Racing Sports Car.
French: Voiture Sport de Course.
German: Rennsportwagen.
Italian: Vettura Sport da Corsa.

Rear-entrance Tonneau

The combined constructional elements of the early type of front-engined Touring Car—a short wheelbase and very large rear wheels or chain rear-wheel drive—necessitated in almost all the early Tonneau cars entrance to the rear seats (the Tonneau) through a rear central door. For further particulars, *see* ^{2}*Tonneau*.

→ ^{2}*Tonneau*

Reise-Coupé

German for Gran Turismo.
→ *Gran Turismo*

Rear-entrance Tonneau. Entry and exit were not easy in this configuration.

Reise-Limousine

German for Berline de Voyage/Touring Limousine.

→ *Berline de Voyage; Touring Limousine*

Rennwagen

German for Racing Car.
→ *Racing Car*

Ribassato

Italian for a low-built or Underslung chassis, usually if not always resulting in a low bodywork style.
→ *Surbaissé; Underslung*

Roadster

The term Roadster has seen a very long history of use which has not always been clear and distinct. The first period was the Horse-Roadster; next was the Runabout-Roadster period; third was the proper Roadster period; fourth was the sporty Convertible-Roadster; fifth is the sporting car/Sports Car Roadster period.

¹Roadster

Originally an equestrian term; a horse for riding or driving on the road.

²Roadster

An American open, simple and very sporting type of vehicle having only basic bodywork: hood; support for the seat and at the rear a fuel tank; Rumble seat or just a simple tail piece; no doors and no windshield; two seats far back in the chassis or a single bench seat for two persons, alternatively two seats mid-chassis plus, sometimes, a Rumble seat. Initially devoid of any weather protection. Later models sported a simple foldable top.

Origins and history

The two-, or sometimes three-seater Roadsters evolved from the earliest and simplest forms of Buggies, Runabouts and some types of High-wheelers. The origins can be traced via the High-wheeler Buggies of the period ca. 1895 to 1910s and the Runabout.
²Runabout ←

Important period
1905–1920.

Variations

There were many variations of Roadster, as the designs and applications of the term were inconsistent. An alternative, and earlier, term for a Roadster-type vehicle would have been Runabout *(q.v.)*.

³Roadster

An American two or three seater car with two doors, windshield, a small Touring Car style folding top and simple, detachable side-curtains, secured to the body by means of pegs and sockets. Behind the seats was a luggage compartment or Rumble seat *(q.v.)*. Some Roadsters' bodywork were built on the same wheelbase and type of chassis as that of the maker's Touring Car, which resulted in a mid-chassis driver's seat location.

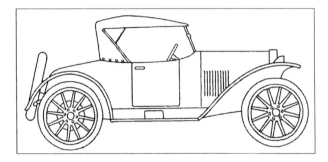

[3]Roadster. The name Roadster has been applied to various styles of more or less sporty vehicles over a long period of time. This illustration represents the middle period, which seems most genuine.

Origins and history

The Roadster with a folding top evolved from the simpler pre–1920 sporting vehicle of the same name.

[2]*Roadster* ←

Important period

1920–1935

Variations

Roadsters came in various degrees of performance and sportiness. The more sedate ones were in effect pre–World War II two- or three-seater Touring Cars; after World War II the term would be used (a trifle inappropriately) for Convertible Coupes *(see below)*. The high-performance Roadster developed into the Speedster. Misleadingly, some manufacturers have applied the Roadster term to four or five seater Touring Cars. However, there are always exceptions to the rule, and the 1918 HAL-Twelve Shamrock Roadster—in spite of being a full four-seater, V12-engined vehicle—by its sporty and very open design, devoid of doors and any weather protection bar windshield and flimsy soft top, fulfilled most of the period criteria for a Roadster.

→ *Speedster;* [1]*Tourer*

[4]Roadster

Starting in about 1930 one variation of the Roadster changed character—by getting roll-down glass side-windows and a tight-fitting soft top. The term Roadster evolved to mean almost the same as a two or three seater non-sporting Convertible Coupe *(q.v.)*. The more sporty *(see above)* version developed into Sports Cars proper, e.g. the Speedster.

European car manufacturers after World War II have often used the term Roadster for their sporting models, probably in an effort to attract overseas customers. Today, the use of this term is spreading, and is intended to denote—almost generally on both sides of the Atlantic—an open sporting car, or, in extreme cases even a pure Sports Car *(q.v.)*.

→ *Convertible Coupe.*

[3]*Roadster* ←

[5]Roadster

Post–World War II sporty and Sports Cars, mainly outside America, have become broadly referred to as Roadsters.

→ [5]*Sports Car*

Roi des Belges

An early elegant and spacious open Tonneau bodywork style with comfortable baroque-style, buttoned seats, commissioned by the Belgian King Leopold II in 1902 and called "Roi des Belges Tonneau de Grand Luxe." This particular vehicle was a side-entrance Tonneau automobile probably with chain-drive, the side-entrance made possible by the expedient of swinging the left front seat outwards to give access to the rear seats. The Roi des Belges coachwork style was subsequently repli-

Roi des Belges. A luxurious Tonneau body style originating with the Belgian Royalty.

cated by many coachbuilders and led eventually via the somewhat simpler Tonneau style Touring Car to the Double Phaeton body style.

→ *Tonneau*

Routière

French for an automobile suitable for covering long distances and at the same time affording its driver and passenger ample comfort.

→ *Grande Routière*

RS

These initials have been employed, usually as subtype designation, by German car manufacturers to indicate Rennsport (German for sports racing).

Rumble seat

In the horse-drawn carriage era as well as in automobiles, a seat or two behind the carriage body or the car passenger compartment proper. In the car a single seat or a bench for two passengers folding under a lid of the rear deck of a two-seater Convertible, Coupé or Runabout. When unoccupied the space could be used for luggage. A popular bodywork style in the period between the two World Wars. An optional item that could be had from some auto manufacturers in the 1920s was a rather rudimentary foldable roof for the Rumble Seat passenger(s).

Origins and history

Spider was the Continental name of the extra seat for the footman or groom in the open behind the body of some styles of horse-drawn carriages (*see* *¹Spider*). The forerunner of the Rumble seat, according to the Classic Car Club of America, was the mother-in-law seat, a single seat attached to the back of a two-seater car. (The term "Mother-in-law seat" may have a German origin— *see Schwiegermuttersitze.*)

Important period

Between the two World Wars.

Language varieties

American: Rumble seat, Jump seat.
British: Dickey seat.
French: Spider.
German: Schwiegermuttersitze.
Italian: Spider.

Rumble Seat Coupe

An American Coupé car with a Rumble seat *(q.v.)*.

→ *³Coupé*

¹Runabout

An early American open, light horse-drawn carriage with four large diameter wheels, some variations of which were also called Buggy.

¹Buggy ←

²Runabout

An American light, open two-seater car with rudimentary bodywork devoid of windshield, top and doors. The engine was mounted under-body at mid-chassis or, later, at the front. Sometimes there was provision for a third passenger in a rear, centrally placed Rumble seat. Later versions around 1910 used to have a Victoria-type folding top. The difference between some late Buggies or High-wheelers and early Runabouts is slight, but generally the Runabouts have a smaller road-wheel diameter.

Origins and history

The origins of this vehicle can be traced via the High-wheeler Buggies of the years around 1900 and the earliest and simplest forms of Cyclecars and early Light cars. Many of the early Runabouts were quite similar to the later and more sophisticated examples of High-wheelers.

High-wheeler ←

Important period

From the end of 19th century to 1915.

Variations

The name Runabout was used variously and haphazardly up to about 1930 on almost any kind of simple open vehicle. Today, the designation Runabout has found a fresh application in the modern electrically powered cars and the so called alternative power vehicles.

→ *²Roadster*

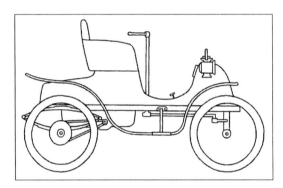

²Runabout. An early under-body engined light American automobile.

-S-

S

This subtype designation has been employed to indicate Super, Sport/Sports, Sprint and Special. The combination SS has been used in Italian to indicate Sprint Speciale and in many languages to denote Super Sport. SL indicates in Italian Superleggera and in German Sport or Super Leicht. The initials SE are intended by some manufacturers to mean Special Edition. In some cases S has been used merely to indicate Sedan bodywork.

→ *Special*

Salamanca

Salamanca has sometimes been used —exclusively on Rolls-Royce chassis— to denote the Cabriolet de Ville bodywork style introduced by Spanish Count Carlos de Salamanca.

Cabriolet de Ville ←

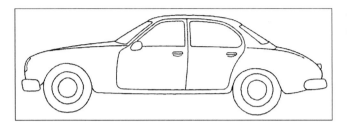

Saloon. The British Saloon is a European Sedan.

Saloon

British for a two- or four-door enclosed owner-driver Four- or Six-light Sedan style of car seating from four to six people, including the driver. To be strict, a Saloon body should have no glass division behind the driver.

Origins and history

The enclosed car was an expensive proposition in the early days of the 20th century. Consistent with improved production methods the cheaper Saloon bodied car—as compared to the more expensive Limousine—became attainable for an ever increasing portion of the community. The term Saloon originates from the railroad all-Pullman saloon car and began to be used around 1910. According to Mclellan, coachbuilders looking for a way to associate their products with the luxury of the Pullman railroad cars found that they would have to pay a royalty for using that name, and so chose the next best word, the Saloon.

Important period

1910 to present.

Variations

A Four-light Saloon (with four side windows) is nowadays often automatically Close-coupled. A somewhat more sporting variation of the Four-light Saloon is the Sports (Sportsman's) Saloon. A Saloon with six side windows, the Six-light Saloon, has usually a greater capacity for passengers or greater legroom for the rear seat passengers. Some coachbuilders are known to have termed examples of their production "Six-light Saloon with division," which constitutes something of a contradiction in terms. "Limousine" would here have been a shorter and perfectly apt name. The rear compartment of a Limousine automobile used to be sometimes referred to as a "Saloon."

→ *3, 4Sedan*

Saloon Landaulet

British for a Landaulet-Limousine type of bodywork in which the division glass was omitted.

2Limousine ←

Saloon Limousine

A British Limousine in which the chauffeur's section in front of the division was completely integrated with the rest of the bodywork was sometimes referred to as a Saloon Limousine. Limousine would have sufficed.

2Limousine ←

Sänfte

German for Sedan Chair.

→ *2Sedan*

Schiebedach

German for Sliding Roof.

→ *Sliding Roof*

Schrägheck-Limousine, fünftürig.

German alternative term for Kombi-Limousine.

→ *Hatchback Sedan*

Schwiegermuttersitze

German for Rumble seat. (This term translates as "mother-in-law seat.")

→ *Rumble seat*

¹Sedan

(Sedan carriage) There are some indications that the name Sedan was first applied to a horse-drawn carriage, but the information is scarce and varied: Angelucci and Bellucci in *The Automobile* show an illustration of an elegant six-light enclosed carriage titled "Panel Sedan (1780)" without textual comment. Sallmann in his *Kutschenlexikon*, however, shows an open carriage which is exhibited in the Napoleon-Museum Arenenberg in Thurgau, Switzerland, and there titled "Sedan-Wagen." This open carriage is for four passengers sitting face-to-face with the coachman's seat in front on a perch and a Spider seat at the back. It does not seem to have a hood or top at all. It is stated that the carriage was built by Ehrler in Paris for Napoléon III when he had to travel in 1870 from the town of Sedan in France to surrender to the (then) Prussian King Wilhelm I and Kanzler Otto von Bismarck. On the other hand, Sedan is not mentioned anywhere by Tarr.

²Sedan

(Sedan chair) The name Sedan was also applied to a portable, elegant and comfortable, usually enclosed means of transportation for one person, carried fore and aft by two ridden horses or two human porters. The Sedan chair enjoyed high status, for only the wealthy could afford to hire or own one. Also, the ride was far more agreeable than that provided by the primitively suspended body on the horse-drawn undercarriages of the period. One highly rated quality of the Sedan chair was the possibility it afforded for the porters to enter a house in inclement weather through the front door and allow the — usually important — passenger entry or exit in comfort.

Origins and history

One theory states that this form of conveyance was invented and also produced in the 17th century town Sedan. According to another, the Sedan term derives from "sedere," Italian for sit.

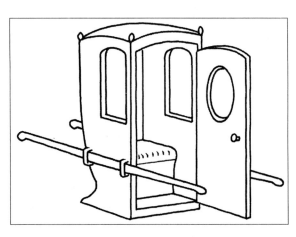

²Sedan chair. A single passenger vehicle carried by either horses or human porters.

The Pope's mobile throne, Sedia Gestatoria, is mentioned by Robertson as an early form of Sedan chair. Whether a Sedan carriage *(¹Sedan)* or Sedan chair has had any influence on the nomenclature of the automobile is not clear.

Important period

17th and 18th century.

Variations

A development of the Sedan chair

was a two-wheeled variant drawn by one man only and called Brouette *(q.v.)*. The Brouette must have enjoyed a very limited popularity with the other Sedan chair porter, who lost his subsistence.

Language varieties
American: Sedan Chair
British: Sedan Chair.
French: Porte-Chaise.
German: Sänfte.
Italian: Carruccio.
→ *Brouette*

³Sedan

(2-door Sedan) The two-door Sedan is the two-door counterpart of the four-door Sedan; i.e., an enclosed car with seating for five to six passengers, including the driver. Like the four-door version it constitutes the normal fixed-roof non-chauffeur driven family or business car with no partition glass and four side windows. The roof length and interior space are equivalent to those of the four-door Sedan version of the same car; the two doors, however, are larger than the front doors of the four-door Sedan.

Origins and history
The normal early two-door four to five passenger vehicle which began to be produced in America in the first half of the 1920s were the Coaches and the more expensive two-door Broughams

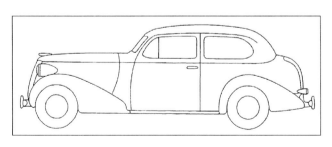

³Sedan. A typical 1930s two-door American Sedan, a bodywork style now extinct.

(see ²Coach, ⁴Brougham). Instead of making a shorter body, like the aforementioned, some American auto manufacturers in the early 1930s found that by eliminating the rear doors of the standard (four-door) Sedan body and modifying the front ones they could rationalize the production of the two-door variation. Thus, apart from different doors and side windows the two-door Sedan was exactly like the four-door car, with the same seating arrangements and other characteristics, but access to the rear seat was via the front doors. Although both Coaches and Broughams were produced by some manufacturers into the 1930s, in practical terms the two-door Sedan superseded the two-door Brougham and the Coach. Whereas the mass-produced four-door Sedan has survived to the present time, its two-door American look-alike disappeared generally after the mid–1960s. Its place—both in the United States and elsewhere—was taken into modern times by the contemporary so-called Coupé *(see ⁴Coupé)*. In Europe, at least a couple of manufacturers kept making the four-door's two-door kin until 1984.

⁴*Sedan* ←
Important period
Ca. 1927 to mid–1960s.
Variations

Except for the full-length 1925 Kurtz and 1926 Jewett, early American two-door vehicles for more than three persons had less passenger space and shorter, Chummy-like bodywork than the vehicle that established itself in the 1930s as the four-door Sedan's look-alike. A few American auto makers in the 1920s applied the name two-door Sedan to their short body two-door cars. One auto maker is known to have changed the name of its two-door Brougham to Sedan for an almost identical two-door vehicle between model years 1924 and 1925. In France the term "Coach" would specify a two-door car with usually a shorter roof than the normal Sedan *(see also [3]Coach and Close-coupled)*.

Language varieties

In spite of its ancestry in Italy or France, the name Sedan is used only in America and a few countries in Europe, among them the Nordic ones. The two-door Sedan in some European countries is alternatively called Coach.

American: Two-door Sedan.
British: Two-door Saloon.
French: Berline à 2 portes, Coach.
German: Limousine or Berline, zwei-türig.
Italian: Berlina 2-porte.

[4]Sedan

(4-door Sedan) By Sedan is essentially meant a four-door enclosed car with seating for five to six passengers, including the driver; i.e., the normal fixed-roof non-chauffeur driven family or business car with four or six side windows and no division glass. In the mid–1930s a luggage compartment became integrated in the bodywork, normally accessible through its own lid at the rear of the car.

Origins and history

Information on horse-drawn carriages called Sedan is scarce and inconsistent. However, it is possible that the Sedan name for car bodywork did originate from the horse-drawn carriage era, likely via the Sedan chair. It has also not been possible as this book goes to press to determine when and why the Sedan epithet went across the Atlantic to become applied in the United States to the bodywork style under consideration. Although the name appeared on a motor vehicle as early as 1914 (the Cole car) it seemed to really catch on in 1916 when several American auto manufacturers used it. According to Locke "The Sedan [in 1918] was just beginning to be recognized as the most convenient form of the automobile ...." The Sedan bodywork in the United States developed more or less parallel with its European counterpart, which originated from the horse-drawn Berline *(q.v.).* From the four-door Sedan evolved during the late 1920s the two-door Sedan, quite similar to the four-door style but with two larger doors and four side windows only *([3]Sedan).*

[3]Berline; [1]Sedan ←

Important period

From the mid–1910s to present.

Variations

A body style that may confuse the issue is the Sedan with left-hand drive and one center entrance door on one side and one or two doors on the other. Such Sedans were produced by some American auto manufacturers in the 1920s. Kissel in 1918 made a "staggered door" Sedan with one front driver's door and one rear door on the curb side. The Business Sedan was a simpler and comparatively rare version produced, according to factory records, periodically after World War II until the early 1960s. A small Sedan: *see Berlinetta.* A sporting Sedan: *see Sports Saloon.* A Sedan-looking car having four doors and a rear hatch door which includes the rear window: *see Hatchback Sedan.* A long wheelbase or lengthened Sedan seating more than six: *see* ²*Limousine and Stretch-limo.*

Language varieties

Having been designated simply Sedan from its inception, when the two-door Sedan turned up the Sedan became increasingly specified as four-door Sedan in the 1930s. In spite of its ancestry in Italy or France, today the name Sedan is used only in America and a few countries in Europe, among them the Nordic ones and Switzerland, the latter within its German speaking part.

American: Sedan.
British: Saloon.
French: Berline.
German: Limousine or Berline.
Italian: Berlina.

Sedanca

Sedanca was the British corresponding name for a Limousine Town Car, a larger variation of the chauffeur-driven Coupé de Ville automobile having either two side windows, one each in the doors of the five to seven seater passenger compartment, or, with the rear Quarters windowed, four side windows. It had a folding canopy for the chauffeur, who would also, on some coach-built variations, be protected by doors. To be strict, the Sedanca bodywork should provide a locker for the folding cant rails and the canopy. Not all Sedancas had this facility. A large proportion of all Sedancas were built by British coachbuilders.

Origins and history

Count Carlos de Salamanca of Madrid, Spain, agent for Rolls-Royce, introduced in 1923 the Sedanca bodywork style, the distinguishing detail being the aforementioned locker for the cant rails and canopy.

Limousine de Ville ←

Important period

The Sedanca was fashionable from the mid–1920s to the late 1930s.

Variations

The large passenger compartment would sometimes, in spite of being enclosed and having a fixed roof, display on its paneled rear Quarters dummy Landau bars (external hood hinge arms) to simulate a Landaulet. An almost similar British bodywork style was the Limousine de Ville, which always had four side windows in the passenger compartment.

Language varieties

Sometimes, and quite unnecessarily, referred to as Sedanca de Ville. For further language varieties, *see Limousine Town Car.*

Sedanca Coupé

The Sedanca Coupé is an elegant variation of the Coupé de Ville body style having only two doors and no division (Walker). It is a strange design when chauffeur driven, for the chauffeur has the easy entry and egress in contrast to his rear seat employer or passenger. A similar bodywork style having a three-position folding top is the *Cabriolet-victoria.*

Important period

1920s to 1930s.

Sedanca de Ville

Variant and superfluous term for Sedanca.

Sedanca ←

Sedan Chair *see* ²Sedan

Sedanet

An American two- and four-door Sedan bodywork variation with a Fastback style rear end treatment. Originally a General Motors name, applied to at least four auto makes.

Origins and history

In 1937 and 1938 Buick produced some variations of two-door Fastback Sedans, whereupon, in 1941, the Sedanet name appeared. It would seem reasonable to presume that Fastbacks were direct predecessors to the Sedanets.

[3]Sedan ←

Important period

Mid–1940s to mid–1950s.

Variations

Some bodywork styles designated Sedanette were produced in the early 1920s and in 1933; see Sedanette.

Sedanette

As early as in the period 1919 to 1922 Lexington in America produced four-door automobiles designated Sedanette, and King, also American, marketed in 1923 a two-door, five-passenger Sedanette. None of these bodies had any hint of the Fastback treatment associated with the much later Sedanet, the King looking in fact like a contemporary two-door Brougham, complete with outside trunk. In 1933 Cadillac produced four-door, five-passenger Sedanettes in the Fleetwood series. It would be reasonable to think that the motivation for the name Sedanette was to indicate a small Sedan body (compare French Berline with the smaller Berlinette and Italian Berlina with Berlinetta [q.v.]). However, it does not appear to have been.

→ Sedanet

Sedan-Limousine

A passage from *The Custom Body Era* by Hugo Pfau defines this style thus: "One variation of this type [Limousine] was one that we at LeBaron, and some other body builders as well, called a Sedan-Limousine. Our own distinction was that a Sedan-Limousine was intended to be driven at least occasionally by the owner. The front compartment was therefore more luxurious than one on a strictly chauffeur-driven car, generally upholstered in the same material used in the rear. We also went to great lengths to make the dividing partition as inconspicuous as possible when the glass was lowered. No customer of ours would admit that he couldn't afford a completely separate car for those occasions when he drove himself."

Selbsttragende Karosserie

German for unitary construction (Monocoque).

→ Unitary construction

Semi Fastback

A Sedan bodywork with a barely discernible Notchback body form.

→ Notchback

[1]Shooting Brake

A British horse-drawn vehicle used for carrying several passengers to shoot plus sporting dogs.

[3, 4]Brake; Wagonette ←

[2]Shooting Brake

A motorized Brake or Station Wagon for essentially the same purpose as above. Later, and with extended usage, the bodywork style and the term Estate Car in Great Britain became generally applied to this type of vehicle. However, Shooting Brake is still sometimes but very purposefully applied to higher class Estate Cars in order to differentiate them from their superficially similar and more mundane brethren.

Language varieties

British: Shooting Brake.

French: Break de chasse.
German: Jagdwagen.
Italian: Vettura da caccia.
→ *¹Estate Car*

Single

An obsolete British term used in combination with a bodywork name, e.g. Brougham, Coupé or Landaulet, to denote that the body was coachbuilt without quarter-lights (windows in the rear Quarters) contrary to a Three-quarter body (having the full Sedanca Coupé complement of four or six side windows). The terms Single and Three-quarter were contemporary in the period between the two World Wars. For illustrations, *see e.g. ²Landaulet and Three-quarter.*

→ *Quarter; Three-quarter*

Six-light Saloon

British for a normal British Sedan automobile with six side windows (as opposed to Four-light bodywork, which has usually a shorter roof, smaller interior space and only four side windows). The Six-light Saloon used to have greater legroom for the rear seat passengers. This is not always the case in popular family-size Sedan-style cars today, where the rearmost side windows tend to get ever smaller.

→ *Saloon*

Skiff

A sporting, often open, automobile typically with a rounded rear Boattail bodywork style. The bodywork was usually of lightweight construction, often having the rear portion in wood, boat deck style, as well as various other parts such as the body sides around the passenger compartment. "Skiff" refers often to the complete bodywork, not just the rear section, but is occasionally used as a complementary term in combination (e.g., "Skiff Torpédo") to describe a French Torpedo-style Tourer with Skiff rear end treatment.

Origins and history

The name originated with the boat style tail, at least partly made of wood. From time to time styles and materials from the sailing boat hull were adopted, mostly by coachbuilders, for car bodywork. In particular, the tail treatment lent itself well to be transposed into the bodywork of the open post–World War I car with sporty aspirations.

Important period

1920s and 1930s

Language varieties

In car bodywork context Skiff has been used in France as an alternative term to Bateau or Boattail. (To be strict, the Bateau tail is pointed, not rounded like the Skiff.) The Boattail name seems to have been favored by the Anglo-Americans.

American: Boattail.
British: Boat-tail.
French: Skiff, Bateau, Pointe Bateau.
German: Bootsheck.
Italian: Bateau, Coda Bateau.
→ *Bateau; Boattail; Bordino*

Skiff Torpédo

A not unusual French bodywork designation in the 1920s to specify the combination of a Torpédo general bodywork outline with a rounded tail. (All kinds of bodywork style term combinations were used in the period between the two World Wars, some coachbuilders even compounding three terms together—with dubious effects of clarity.)

→ *Skiff; Torpédo*

SL

Subtype designation indicating Superleggera in Italian or Sport/Super Leicht in German. *See L and S.*

Sliding Roof

An opening roof design, where a rigid panel in the roof of a two- or four-door Saloon-bodied car can be slid backwards to open a part of the roof. The opening, however, is smaller than that of a Sunshine Saloon *(q.v.),* since more than just the cant-rails of the bodywork, and also the rear part of the roof including the rear window, remain in situ.

Language varieties
American: Sunroof.
British: Sliding Roof.
French: Toit ouvrant.
German: Schiebedach.
Italian: Tetto apribile.
→ *Sunshine Saloon*

¹Special

This designation, or its abbreviation S, has been used to denote a home-built car using as a rule various components, both body and chassis, from other cars, or a standard car modified from its original specification. In the words of the late English motorsport journalist Denis Jenkinson the name "Special" "applies to one-off cars that are the product of the fertile brain of the constructor. It is probably true to say that no special has ever been finished! ... If the special builder ever says his car is finished, it will usually indicate that it is now obsolete and he is starting on a new one." The bodywork of the home-built Special has seldom been noted for its outstanding beauty.

²Special

An official model name given by a (usually American) auto manufacturer.
→ *S*

Speedster

Genuinely American term for an open and fast two-seater Sports Car, often with a Boattail bodywork style.

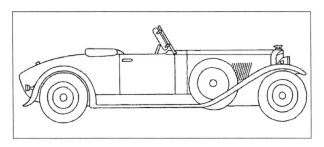

Speedster. Many of the 1930s American Speedster automobiles were extremely handsome vehicles.

With a few exceptions (in 1914 and 1929) pre–World War II Speedsters were produced on fairly long wheelbase chassis and had bodyworks of very nice proportions providing a near mid-chassis (between wheel axles) seating position. Bodyworks of American two-seater front-engined Sports Cars after World War II, although not always termed Speedsters, have usually approached the European seating position closer to the (driven) rear wheels.

Origins and history
Speedsters were the 1930s sporty version of the earlier Roadster. The term Speedster seems to have been used by reputable American car manufacturers initially in the decades prior to World War II as an alternative denomination to both Runabout and the time-honored (but later to become gradually less sporty) Roadster term for quite large two-seater Sports Cars.
³Roadster ←

Important period
Ca. 1915 to present.

Variations

A few coachbuilders, mainly in the 1930s, did construct some four-door automobiles designated Speedsters. After World War II some European Sports Car manufacturers have appropriated, or attempted to appropriate, the name Speedster, but the cars have very little except performance in common with their original American namesakes. It can be assumed that the original idea was to attract transatlantic customers.

Language varieties

American: Sport Car, Speedster, Sports Car.

British: Sports Car.

French: Voiture Sport, Spider.

German: Sportwagen.

Italian: Vettura Sport, Spider.

→ *¹, ²Sports Car*

¹Spider

The term Spider was used in France and other European countries to denote the extra rear groom seat, or bench, on spidery outriggers behind the driver's and passenger's seat proper of some early, very light, short wheelbase, horse-drawn carriages. Subsequently the complete carriages—which were often variations of the Phaeton carriage—were termed Spider. *See ¹Phaeton*.

²Spider

Early automobiles inherited both the Spider seat and the term; thus Spider was originally the French and Italian term for a Rumble seat, but subsequently became used to denote complete cars. The Spider seat was for the groom/mechanician, who had to attend to the needs of

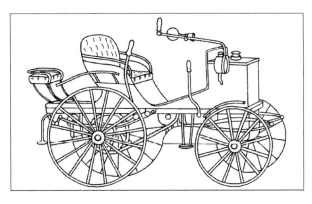

²Spider. The Spider seat gave the whole vehicle the name Spider, later to be applied even to two-seater Sports Cars.

¹Spider. The early "Spider" was in actual fact a Phaeton style carriage with a rear Spider (Rumble) seat.

the early motor vehicle proprietor and the automobile: crank-starting the engine, changing tires (frequently), cleaning etc. Some of the very early ones were primitive (for illustration, *see ²Spider*). In the beginning of the previous century heavier and more luxurious two-seater vehicles were coachbuilt with a foldable Victoria-style top, and as late as in the early 1920s even a few four-door Double Phaetons with a fifth rearmost central seat for the *mécanicien* are known to have been constructed. In the period around World War I the Spider name was also applied to the sporty owner-driver's very light and spidery cars having no Spider seat. These vehicles had maximum two-seater (sometimes even single-seater) bodywork and no fenders (wings) or at most only small cycle-type ones close to the wheels. They can be considered a cross-over between the Cyclecar and the Sports Car, and the term Spider in this connotation is still being used (*Spider, below).

³Spider

French and Italian for Rumble seat.
→ *Rumble seat*

⁴Spider

A contemporary open *pukka (q.v.)*, light two-seater Sports Car (sometimes spelled Spyder). In present day American English, Italian and French usually denotes a modern open two-seater Sports Car.
→ *¹Sports Car*

Sport

"Sport" in connection with motor vehicles is a term to indicate sporting qualities like good performance and simple, preferably two-seater bodywork. Applied to quite non-sporting, enclosed cars in addition to or in combination with a main model designation, "Sport" has been used by many manufacturers to denote implied sporting propensities. In extreme cases car manufacturers have added "Sport" to the main model name of catalogue Sedan cars with completely standard bodywork, the supposedly sporting touch coming from some petty extra horsepower, special wheels or "go faster" stripes. In cases, however,

where e.g. a Sedan version really has been made lighter, better handling and nimbler, and therefore more sporting, this addition to the normal model name could possibly be justified, but "Ti" would here be an excellent alternative with a provenance.
→ *Sports Car; Ti*

Sport Car

Alternative (and unusual) American term for Sports Car.
→ *Sports Car*

Sportcoupé

German for Sports Coupé.
→ *Sports Coupé*

¹Sports Car

A traditional *pukka (q.v.)* Sports Car is an open, light front-engined rear-wheel drive two-seater car with simple bodywork, a basic folding top and simple removable side-screens, with or without two doors, with seats well back in the car close to the rear wheels, designed for speed and maneuverability but with the importance rather more on agility than absolute engine power.

²Sports Car

The somewhat less traditional Sports Car is an open, light, two-door either mid- or rear-engined two-seater vehicle with simple bodywork, a canvas fold-

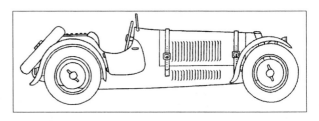

¹Sports Car. British style.

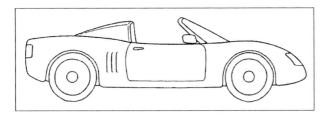
²**Sports Car. A modern mid-engined example.**

ing top and simple detachable side-screens. Seats as close to the engine room as possible. Designed for speed and maneuverability.

³Sports Car

Any enclosed fixed-top, light, front-, mid- or rear-engined car that otherwise fulfills either definition above, designed for speed and maneuverability. Such a fixed-top two-door Sports Car would best and most appropriately be termed a Sport Coupe or Sports Coupé.

→ *Sport Coupe, Sports Coupé*

⁴Sports Car

A limited production open sporty Supercar with two-door bodywork and a very powerful engine, designed for speed, performance and maneuverability *(see also Supercar)*.

⁵Sports Car

The contemporary Sports Car is usually a comparatively heavy but powerful open or enclosed, front- or rear-engined, two-seater or Two-plus-two car with modern non-pukka electric and electronic comforts, including Cabriolet-like tight-fitting top and glass wind-up windows, a sound system and even various power-driven accessories. It is, though, designed for speed and maneuverability, and in some quarters and countries is referred to as Roadster.

Origins and history

Almost all very early motor vehicles were unintentionally extremely sporting on account of their general primitiveness and, except for the occasional Victoria top, complete lack of weather protection. Subsequently, bodyworks became increasingly weather-tight and efficient in shutting out inclement weather. This made the simple, traditionally styled sporty vehicle without comforts and fixed top—the true Sports Car—attractive, which accounts for the fact that some people still prefer it. In its purest form the pukka Sports Car is open, austere and nippy and has no unnecessary decorations or ornamentation outside or inside. The emphasis is on performance, excellent handling, precise steering, rear-wheel drive and unpretentious bodywork. Until approximately World War II the engine did not have to be extremely powerful, whereas subsequently the accent on power and performance has tended to increase. Futile in a Sports Car are automatic functions, comforts and stereo systems. A canvas fold-down top and simple removable side-screens are considered sufficient for weather protection by the Sports Car enthusiast. There is no harm at all in beautiful bodywork, but it is by no means a criterion.

Important period

1910s to present.

Variations

In the United States Runabout denotes an early very simple and sporting vehicle, whereas Speedster is an apposite contemporary term for a Sports Car. The Roadster was originally sporty but became later less so. Some modern

American Sports Cars seat two or three rear passengers comfortably, and some European vehicles two. Some Sports Cars can be had with a removable Hardtop in addition to the regular rag top *(see ²Hardtop)*. Targa *(q.v.)* is an internationally used Italian term for a disguised roll-over bar, which lends its name to the complete car and makes an open Sports Car somewhat less open. In certain cases the Targa bar allows the fitting of roof panels to form a closed vehicle. (For open sporting cars with space for several passengers—*see Sports Tourer, Torpédo, Two-plus-two.*)

Language varieties

Unmistakable terms for pukka Sports Cars are the almost international Spider *(q.v.)* (sometimes spelled Spyder) and the Italian Barchetta *(q.v.)*, which is perhaps best known among the Sports Car *cognoscenti*. Sportster was a term used in some connections in America for a period shortly after World War II. In France and Italy, to describe a pukka open Sports Car, the subtype designation GS or Gran Sport (in Italian) and Grand Sport (in French) used to be popular particularly in the period 1920–1960. In France in the 1920s Torpédo was a normal term for open cars, some of which in two-seater form were indeed Sports Cars. After World War II the American term Roadster has taken on a somewhat more sporting significance, especially in Germany but also elsewhere in Europe, where pure Sports Cars are sometimes referred to and advertised as Roadsters. "Cabrio" in Germany and "Aperto" in Italy are used generally for open cars and could sometimes infer a Sports Car. Today, the term Sports Car has become accepted—in many quarters apparently without hesitation—for some modern open sporting vehicles having all-weather protection and power accessories.

American: Speedster, Sport Car, Sports Car.

British: Sports Car.

French: Voiture Sport, Spider.

German: Sportwagen.

Italian: Vettura Sport, Spider.

Sport Coupe, Sports Coupé

A Sports Coupé denotes a *pukka* enclosed Sports Car; i.e., any front-, mid- or rear-engined vehicle having essentially a fixed-head two-seater bodywork which fulfills the criteria (except folding top) of a sports car *(see ¹⋅²Sports Car)*. Rarely, a Sports Coupé could include one or two minimal rear seats. The distinctive difference between a normal, non-sporting Coupé and a rear-wheel driven Sports Coupé is obvious from the driver's position: In the Sports Coupé the driver and passenger sit as close as possible to the driving rear wheels, whereas in the normal contemporary Coupé the driver and passenger sit farther forward (mid-chassis) in the car, with provision for two or even three rear seat passengers. Even without specifying open top or enclosed it would be correct to call a Sports Coupé a Sports Car.

Origins and history

Although by no means unknown before 1940, the Sports Coupé appeared in significant numbers only after World War II, when some modern sporting drivers called for the comfort of enclosure combined with the sporting qualities of the true open Sports Car. Porsche cars, which were conceptually enclosed from the beginning, contributed substantially to this evolution.

Important period

Early 1950s to present.

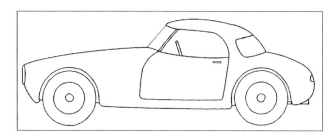

Sports Coupé. An enclosed Sports Car.

Variations

A Sports Coupé lengthened to seat four people *(see Two-plus-two).* Modern Sports Coupés have as a rule electric and electronic comforts and full stereo sound systems. A fact that is obvious to all Sports Car enthusiasts is that these distracting appliances do not add at all to the driving pleasure. The term Coupé, sometimes used in this connection, is inadequate, as it could infer a non-sporting vehicle. *See also Supercar.*

Language varieties

American: Sport Coupe, Sports Coupe.
British: Sports Coupé.
French: Coupé (Grand) Sport.
German: Sportcoupé.
Italian: Coupé (Gran) Sport.
➙ [1, 2, 3]*Sports Car*

Sports Saloon

The British term Sports Saloon, originally Sportsman's Saloon, denotes a car which is lighter and faster than a normal Saloon. In addition, its Close-cou-

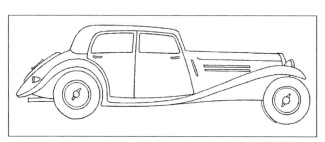

Sports Saloon. A British pre–World War II Sports Saloon.

pled bodywork usually has a sporting style.

Important period

1920s to present.

Language varieties

American: Sport Sedan.
British: Sportsman's or Sports Saloon.
French: Berline Sport.
German: Sportinnenlenker.
Italian: Berlina Sport.
➙ *Close-coupled Saloon*

Sportster

American alternative term, unusual today, for a sporty car or a Sports Car.
➙ [4]*Roadster;* [1]*Sports Car*

Sports Tourer

A Touring Car with enhanced performance. Several of the famous high-quality and efficient British Tourers from the twenties are very sporting Sports Tourers. The nearest American term would be Sport Touring, but actual specimens were few—only some Dual-cowl Sport Phaetons and very rare coachbuilt four-door Speedsters. An American advanced style Sport Touring Car is described and illustrated under *Underslung.*

Important period

1920–1950.

Language varieties

American: Sport Touring.
British: Sports Tourer.
French: Torpédo Grand Sport or Grand Sport.
German: Sporttourenwagen.
Italian: Torpèdo Gran Sport or Gran Sport.
➙ *Touring Car*

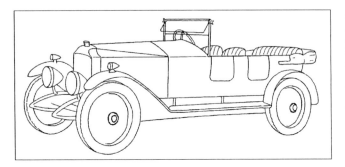

Sports Tourer. The best British Sports Tourers were produced in the 1920s.

Sporttourenwagen

German for Sports Tourer.
→ *Sports Tourer*

Sport Touring

American for Sports Tourer.
→ *Sports Tourer; Underslung*

Sport-utility Vehicle

Full name for SUV.
→ *SUV*

Sportwagen

German for Sports Car.
→ *Sports Car*

Springfield top

An American tight-fitting soft top for Convertible automobiles. *(See All-weather.)*

Spyder

Fairly common way of spelling Spider. Spider is the correct and original Italian and French spelling.
→ *Spider*

Stadt-Limousine

German for Coupé de Ville.
Coupé de Ville ←

Stadt-Limousine, 4-fenstrig

Stadt-Limousine, 4-fenstrig, in German meant a large Coupé de Ville with

enclosed luxurious compartment for five to seven passengers, usually with foldable forward facing extra seats. The passenger compartment was characterized by having four side windows. Always chauffeur driven. The chauffeur's seat was in the open with the possibility to pull forward or to fix a canopy. The bodywork of this type of automobile was mostly coachbuilt. For illustration, *see Coupé Limousine.*

Origins and history

Later, when the chauffeur was allowed the comfort of complete enclosure, the vehicle, still with a glass division, became a Limousine.
Stadt-Limousine ←
Important period
1920–1935.
→ *Limousine Town Car*

Stahlfaltdach-Cabrio

Contemporary German term for a two- or a four-seater open two-door car with a retractable hard metal roof which, with power assistance, can be folded and stowed into the trunk, thereby making it in effect a Convertible car. With the roof closed the top is well insulated and the external visual impression is that of a fully enclosed Coupe.
→ *²Coupé-cabriolet*

¹Stanhope

The first Stanhope horse-drawn vehicle was a Gig made in the beginning of the 19th century for English clergyman Fitzroy Stanhope (1787–1864). It was a light, open two-wheeled horse-drawn carriage for two persons with a seat having fairly high, banister-like elbow and back rests. It had no top. After 1880 fresh interest in this type of carriage had it named Buggy both in England and in France (Sallmann). A later variation was the four-wheeled Stanhope Phaeton with front and rear seats and a Victoria style top for the front seat, which was fairly similar to the banistered seat of the two-wheeled Stanhope. The rear seat was of simpler execution.

[2]Stanhope

The motor Stanhope was an American two-seater vehicle, the body of which was modeled on the simple lines of its horse-drawn forerunner. The four-wheeled chassis contained usually an under-body internal-combustion engine, but some utilized electric or steam propulsion. Steering was mostly by tiller and some sported a Victoria-type top. Most early Stanhopes had thin High-wheeler-style wheels, and these could be found on some vehicles right up to 1908. Usually the later Stanhope cars—which were sometimes termed Runabouts—utilized motorcycle-like wire-wheels with thin tires, which were

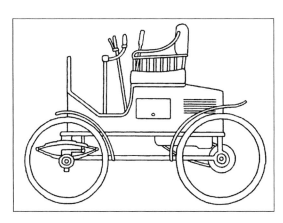

[2]Stanhope. There were certain similarities between the Stanhope and the early Runabout.

normal for light motor vehicles of the period.

Important period
1898–1910.

State Coach

A heavy and luxurious horse-drawn formal Coach primarily used for state and gala occasions. Designs vary.
Carrozza ←

Station Wagon

An American enclosed three- or (more commonly) five-door vehicle usually based on the normal production Sedan but having the roof extended backwards to form an enclosed and spacious rear compartment to seat up to nine passengers, having the rear gate or door usually designed in two halves, the upper of which is hinged transversely at its upper edge and the lower half side-hinged or transversely hinged at its bottom edge. Rear seats can be folded forward or removed to considerably increase the carrying space. According to Flammang and Kowalke the three-door wagon often has sliding or flip-out rear side windows and quite a few of the five-door versions have retained simulated wood paneling, keeping alive the wagon's origin as a wood-bodied vehicle.

Origins and history

The original Station Wagon vehicle with bodywork built of wood derived from the early horse-drawn Bronson Wagon, of which the Brewster Co. produced its own version around 1900. The Brewster wagon was distinguished by its wooden body featuring overlaid, narrow and contrasting wooden strips laid out in a rectangular pattern like mullioned windows

Station Wagon. An early Station Wagon from the period around World War I.

(Andy Rheault). The first American car manufacturer to produce an automotive version, fitted to a 1915 Ford model T, was J.T. Cantrell & Co. (D. & K. Chapman). The body of this vehicle had a long roof and three rows of seats, low doors and simple roll-down side curtains for weather protection. Around World War I these Station Wagons with wooden bodies were referred to as "Depot Wagons" and were chiefly employed for taking people to and from the railway station, carrying goods to the train depot, commuting to the city for work or similar purposes. Later Station Wagons were constructed of steel.

Important period
USA: 1915 to 1995.
Outside USA: 1930s to date.

Station Wagon. The European Station Wagon has a shorter rear overhang than its American, now almost obsolete, counterpart.

Variations
The American Station Wagon in the post–World War II period grew to very large size, but has now in the United States been largely superseded by the Minivan (*q.v.*) and the SUV (*q.v.*). A New England variation of the Station Wagon theme was the Beach Wagon. Outside North America Station Wagons are smaller and are either three-door (two-door plus tailgate or lift-up hatch) or five-door (four-door plus tailgate or lift-up hatch). Seating capacity is up to seven. A further variation is the mix between a Coupé or Sedan and Station Wagon constituting the smaller Hatchback Coupe and Hatchback Sedan (*q.v.*).

Language varieties
After World War II the pre-war wooden Station Wagon acquired the colloquial name Woodie, which is frowned upon in certain quarters. Station Wagon is, even in some formal contexts, sometimes abbreviated to just Wagon. The basically American term Station Wagon is being used in many countries outside the United States both colloquially and formally (applied in sales literature and even as a trade name by quite a few car manufacturers).

American: Station Wagon.
British: Estate Car.
French: Break and Familiale.
German: Kombi or Kombiwagen.
Italian: Familiare, Break, Station Wagon.
→ *Beach Wagon; Minivan; SUV*

Streamline

Term to describe a streamlined body-work.

American: Streamline.
British: Streamline.
French: Profilé.
German: Stromlinienform.
Italian: Aerodinamica.

Streitwagen

German for a Chariot for war and hunting.

→ *Chariot*

Stretch-limo

Stretch-limo is short for a stretched Limousine; a basically American very long enclosed, comfortable chauffeur-driven multi-passenger vehicle, often with division glass. It has four or six doors, but when employed by hotels and airline companies usually six. Passenger capacity is around nine, sometimes with rear facing bench front seats in the passenger compartment.

Origins and history

One of the earliest vehicles for triumphal state occasions was the Chariot; later, for state or gala occasions, the heavy horse-drawn formal Coach (Carrozza) came into use. Whereas for the latter purpose the horse-drawn Coach is still used in a few countries, Stretch-limousines in both enclosed and open form are being used in others. An additional use for the Stretch-limo is passenger conveyance by corporations, airline companies and hotels. An earlier and unpretentious American body style variation of this vehicle was the Parlor Coach, superseded, after a lengthy interval, by the Passenger Van.

Carrozza; Chariot; ²Limousine ←

Important period

The requirement of luxurious ceremonial automobiles for state and gala occasions combined with more passenger space than that offered by the standard family size car has always existed. Stretch-limo: 1930s to present.

Variations

Bullet-proof bodies with division glass are especially favored for state occasions and by company executives. European very long Limousines are usually lengthened versions of existing production Sedan bodied cars, although a few auto makers have been known to manufacture Stretch-limos as series production vehicles. An extra long Stretch-limo is the Super Stretch-limo. A present day open version is the Convertible or Cabriolet Stretch-limousine. Some Stretch-limos for heads of state are designed with a rear section Landaulet-style folding top.

Language varieties

In England Humber used to call their

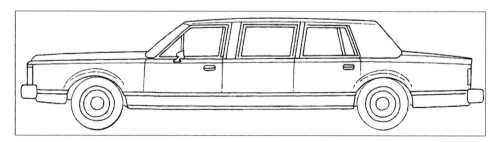

Stretch-limo. The four-door and six-door Stretch-limo is produced in much larger quantities in America than elsewhere.

extra long limousine Pullman Limousine (*see Saloon.*) In France even an elongated Limousine used to be called Limousine, whereas the tendency is that the term Stretch-limo is gaining popularity in Europe. In Germany a long Limousine is normally termed Pullman-Limousine but after World War II a very long Pullman-Limousine has become generally termed Gestreckte Limousine or Stretch-Limo. In Italy an extra long Limousine with division would be termed Limousine allungata, one without division Berlina allungata.

American: Stretch-limo.

British: Stretch-limousine.

French: Stretch Limousine or Stretch-limo.

German: Gestreckte Limousine, Stretch-Limo.

Italian: Limousine allungata, Berlina allungata (without division).

➡ *Airport Limousine; Convertible Stretch-limo; Passenger Van; Super Stretch-limo*

Stretch-limo Décapotable

French for Convertible Stretch-limo.

➡ *Convertible Stretch-limo*

Stretch-limousine

Full name, used both in Britain and France for Stretch-limo.

➡ *Stretch-limo*

Stromlinienform

German for streamlined bodywork.

➡ *Profilé*

Stufenheck

German for Notchback.

➡ *Notchback*

Suburban

Name appearing infrequently and inconsistently during a long period of time as applied by American auto manufacturers. According to one source Suburban implies a seven passenger Limousine; that is contradicted, however, by the following examples of vehicles given this designation: a few Sedan-style automobiles in the first decade of the 20th century; some Coach- and Sedan-style models in the 1920s; one Station Wagon in the 1960s; and a large Off-roader or (in later terminology) SUV from the 1930s to the present.

Sunroof

A comparatively rare body style in America, consisting of a rigid sliding or folding top that can be raised over the bridge beam side rails above the doors. One auto manufacturer in the 1950s rather confusingly termed a car so configured a "Convertible Landau"; another used the phrase "Skytop." Further details and illustration can be found under *Cabrio-Limousine. See also Sunshine Saloon.*

Sunshine Saloon

A British two- or four-door Saloon with fully or partly folding, soft "sunshine" roof having stationary cant-rails, i.e., the side-window/door frames remained fixed when the roof was folded or slid back. The rear window also remained usually fixed. The Continental style of soft, folding roof style was characterized by the folding rear window which left the back open (for illustration, *see Cabrio-Limousine*).

Origins and history

The desire to travel by car in good weather with no roof to hinder the rays of sun seems to have been both normal and important, particularly in the early days of 20th century motoring. In Europe, the Touring Car became for some too primitive, and even the later Cabriolet or Drop-head Coupé did not offer quite the combination of open air and good protection afforded by the framed windows. This led to the popularity of the soft, folding Sunshine roof style of middle class popular family automobiles.

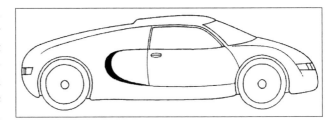

Supercar. This Supercar is an enclosed mid-engined, extremely high-speed Sports Coupé.

All-weather ←

Important period

Approximately mid–1920s to World War II.

Variations

The American term Sunroof could imply a folding as well as a rigid Sliding Roof *(q.v.)*. On the Continent, and especially in Germany, France and Italy, the soft, fully folding or roll-down roof usually included the rear window.

Language varieties

An alternative British name was sometimes Saloon Cabriolet (Walker).

American: Sunroof.

British: Sunshine Saloon.

French: Découvrable or Voiture Découvrable.

German: Cabrio- or Kabrio-Limousine *(q.v.)*

Italian: Berlina a tetto apribile.

Supercar

A limited production extremely powerful, high performance open or enclosed two- or (sometimes) four-seater modern car. Front- or mid-engined and usually rear wheel driven, Supercars very seldom have four doors, though they are often comfortable and sometimes even luxurious. Open cars of generally similar style but strictly two-seaters, minus luxury and luggage space: *see ⁴Sports Car*. Enclosed specimens that meet the criteria of comfort, space for luggage and luxury could reasonably be termed modern Gran Turismo vehicles. (For enclosed cars of generally similar style but from an earlier era with an accent more on comfort than performance, *see ¹Gran Turismo*.)

Super Stretch-limo

An American extra long Limousine, longer than a Stretch-limo. Seats 12–14 passengers.

→ *Stretch-limo*

Surbaissé

This is a French chassis term that affects bodywork. Surbaissé means lowered. A consequence of a lowered chassis is very often, if not always, a low body style, which has led to the application of this term, in normal parlance, to describe a low-built bodywork.

Language varieties

American: Low Chassis, Underslung.

British: Low Chassis, Underslung.

French: Surbaissé.

German: Tiefergelegt.

Italian: Ribassato.

→ *Low-chassis*

¹Surrey

Originally the Surrey Cart was a two-wheeled horse-drawn carriage. The name sprang from the English county by that name, and an example was imported to the United States in the 1860s. There a carriage builder took it as a pattern for modification and adaptation into a light four-wheeled carriage which was characterized by two or three rows of similar seats with easy entry and egress. Very often this style of carriage was equipped with a roof, a so called Surrey top, standing on light pillars (Sallmann).

²Surrey

Bodywork style of an American early automobile embodying the same characteristics as its predecessor carriage; two rows of similar seats usually under a roof on pillars but sometimes having an extended foldable top. There were no doors and very seldom any windshield.

The four-wheeled chassis contained usually an under-body internal-combustion engine, but some utilized electric propulsion. Steering was mostly by tiller and some sported a shorter Victoria-style top. Irrespective of period, Surrey vehicles had either delicate Highwheeler style wheels or smaller diameter

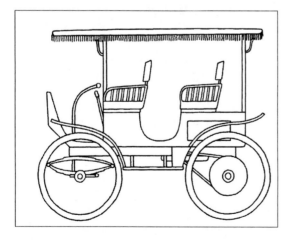

²Surrey. The Surrey motor vehicle was a four-seater (as opposed to some contemporary two-seaters, e.g. the Stanhope).

wire-spoke wheels shod with thin pneumatic tires.

Important period
1900–1910.
Variations
Surrey was also the brand name of an American late 1950s replica production of the 1903 "curved dash" Oldsmobile.

SUT

Abbreviation for Sport-utility Truck. A four-door enclosed vehicle first presented in 1999, combining a comfortable full five or six seater SUV-class passenger compartment with a pick-up truck rear end, the former setting it apart from the more utilitarian Dual-cab (crew cab) type of pick-up vehicle. All four wheels are either permanently engaged (driven) or one or the other pair of wheels can be disengaged at the driver's discretion.
SUV ←
Important period
2000 to present.
→ *Off-roader*

SUV

Abbreviation for Sport-utility Vehicle. A comfortable, high-roofed, usually enclosed Station Wagon type three- or five-door vehicle with off-road propensities (to varying degrees), high ground clearance and good facilities for hauling people and sporting equipment. All four wheels are either permanently engaged (driven) or one or the other pair of wheels can be disengaged at the driver's discretion. The rear gate is top- or side-hinged (often with an outside spare wheel) or divided. A few manufacturers produce an open three-door, heavily roll

SUV. The Sport-utility Vehicle has nearly ousted the Station Wagon in America, but not yet in Europe.

barred version having either a soft top or removable Hardtop *(see ²Hardtop).*

Station Wagon ←

Origins and history

The origins are a Station Wagon type of body combined with off-road power transmission provisions. A characteristic for this type of vehicle is that the wheelbase of the three-door bodywork version is usually shorter than that of the five-door. In the United States the SUV and the Minivan *(q.v.)* have largely superseded the Station Wagon.

Important period

Ca. 1990 to present.

Variations

The open, usually short wheelbase sporty versions normally have fixed door- and window-frames (Sunshine Saloon-style). A European SUV is normally somewhat smaller than its American counterpart and would probably be termed Compact. An SUV with pickup rear end: *see SUT.*

Language varieties

In the Far East the abbreviation RV, denoting Recreational Vehicle, is sometimes used for this type of vehicle.

American: Sport-utility or SUV.

British: SUV.

French: Gros Break 4x4 or 4x4 de Loisir.

German: Geländekombi or S.U.V.

Italian: SUV (colloquially also Fuoristrada).

→ *Off-roader*

-T-

¹T

Classical abbreviation for Turismo or Touring, usually in combination with G to form GT.

→ *GT*

²T

In recent decades frequently applied by manufacturers as a subtype designation for Turbo, to indicate a forced induction system by means of an exhaust gas driven turbocharger.

Targa, Targa-top

A disguised roll-over bar, making an open Sports Car somewhat less open, as it were, but safer. The term derives from Targa Florio competition cars. In certain cases the Targa bar allows the fitting of roof panels to form a closed vehicle.

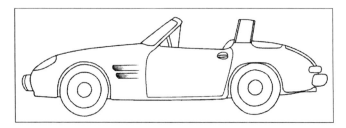

Targa. The Targa-top bodywork style has been utilized in front-as well as mid- and rear-engined Sports Cars.

Sports Car ←
Important period
1960s to 1980s.
Language varieties
Targa, as a bodywork style and a vehicle type, is internationally known.
Italian: T-roof.
→ *T-roof; T-top*

Taxi (Taxi-cab, Taxicab)

An enclosed four- to six-seater automobile equipped with a taximeter and other accouterments for transporting people to a specified destination and charging them a fare, normally depending on the distance traveled. Outside Great Britain, the contemporary Taxi automobile is often a standard production Sedan or Minivan (MPV). In the United States SUVs also do service as Taxis, and Stretched Sedans and Taxi Limousines for up to nine passengers exist.

Origins and history
The term Taxi traces its origins from the Greek "táxis" and "táttein" (to regulate, arrange and further to charge). The vehicle originated in the horse-drawn era, when horse-drawn Cabriolets, or "Cabs," were used as public service vehicles for transporting people. The term for the instrument for recording distance and calculating cost, the taximeter (taxameter/taxamètre/tassametro etc. in various European languages), became subsequently used to designate the complete vehicle. In the United States taximeter cab became shortened to Taxi, whereafter this abridgment spread more or less internationally. The chequered beltline band to denote a Taxi, very common between the two World Wars, is seen only rarely today.

Cab; Droschke; Fiacre; Hansom Cab
←

Important period
1910–present.
Variations

The variations of vehicles and their body styles manufactured over the years for the sole purpose of transporting people for pay are manifold. The British and Continental European 1920s Taxi was mostly of the Landaulet body style; i.e., the rearmost Quarter roof behind the passenger compartment doors of the body was

Taxi. A 1920s purpose-built Taxi exhibiting the classic checkered belt-line band.

collapsible *(see Landaulet-Fiacre)*. In the United States Taxis used to be special vehicles usually built by well-known auto manufacturers *(see illustration)*. British Taxis are noted for having employed purposefully sensible bodywork for a great many years.

Language varieties

Today, Taxi has become an internationally used term. In spite of being for all intents and purposes Taxis, in some countries 7–9 passenger stretched Taxi vehicles are called Limousines.

American: Cab, Taxi. *British*: Cab (Taxicab, Taxi).

French: Taxi-auto, Taxi (Taxi-cab). *German*: Taxi, Droschke (arch.). *Italian*: Tassi, taxi.

Three-box

Alternative term for Notchback, applicable in American English, English and Italian.
→ *Notchback*

Three-door Hatchback

British for Hatchback Coupe.
→ *Hatchback Coupe*

Three-position Drop-head Coupé

British alternative term for Folding Head DHC.
→ *Cabriolet-victoria*

Three-quarter

An obsolete British bodywork term that was applied to various body styles, including Brougham, Landaulet and others. Three-quarter has been variously described as denoting *either* that

the body was coachbuilt with rear Quarter side windows (as a Three-quarter Landaulet, illustrated) *or* that a Three-quarter Landaulet's awning over the driver could be folded away in addition to the rearmost Quarter folding

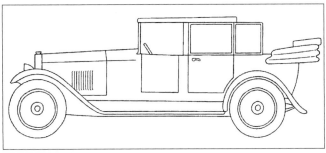

Three-quarter Landaulet. This Landaulet body style has a vast passenger compartment.

top. A Single Landaulet, on the other hand, had only two side windows in the passenger compartment and a rear Quarter folding top.
→ *Quarter; Single*

Three-wheeler

Various terms have been applied to three-wheeled motor vehicles. *See Bubblecars, Cyclecars, Microcars, Tricars and Tricycles.*

Ti, TI

The archetypal Italian abbreviation Ti for Turismo Internazionale has been applied mainly in the period 1960–1980 by Italian and German manufacturers to some of their excellent middlesized sporting Sedans and Berlinas/Berlinettas. (The "i" in some cases is rendered as capital "I.")

Tiefergelegt

German for a low-built (or Underslung) chassis, in consequence of which very often, if not always, a low body-work style resulted.

→ *Low-chassis*

Toit ouvrant

French for Sliding Roof.

→ *Sliding Roof*

[1]Tonneau

A light and low-built, open horse-drawn Cart on two large diameter wheels. One variation, the Governess Car (or Cart, in France), had a space with rounded corners with lengthwise benches for passengers *including* the driver in the rear right corner (Sall-mann). Another variation was a some-what larger carriage having a separate driver's bench in front. Access to the passenger seats in both cases was through a rear central gate.

Origins and history

The first Tonneau carts were built around the end of the 19th century, possibly as a lighter variation of the Wagonette (Blomquist). Both body styles described above cause association to barrel ("tonneau" in French) on ac-count of their round form in the verti-cal plane.

[1]*Car* ←

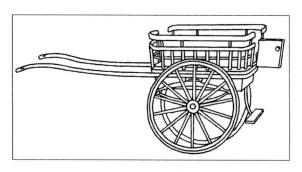

[1]**Tonneau. The Tonneau style Governess Car/Cart was eminently suited to transporting pupils, as the governess-driver could overlook her young passengers from her dri-ving position in the right rear corner.**

[2]Tonneau

A late 19th century open, four to six seater automobile with access to the rear seats (the Tonneau) through a central door at the back (sometimes with a built-in forward facing occasional seat in the door), a practice inherited from the horse-drawn carriage era but also caused by technical considerations *(see further below)*. An automobile having this style of bodywork was sometimes specified as a "Rear-entrance Tonneau." Early specimens had no front doors, and characteristic are the deep armchair, buttoned upholstery-style separate front seats, lest the passenger or driver fall out. In the first years of the 20th cen-tury automobiles began ever more to be utilized not only in fine summer weather but also during other times of the year, necessitating weather protec-tion at least for the rear seat passengers. The Victoria-style folding tops for the rear-entrance vehicles became engi-neering challenges, as there had to be a central opening in the top both in folded and erect positions. (See illus-tration on page 113.) The very early Tonneau—generally for Summer use only—had no folding top.

Origins and history

The early Tonneau or Rear-entrance Tonneau was essen-tially a short-wheelbase vehicle. The rear entrance was occa-sioned initially by the car's very high rear wheels and later—on cars with smaller rear wheels but still chain rear-wheel drive —by the front sprockets of the side drive-chains, which were located on both sides approxi-mately at the place that would have been ideal for entrance to the rear seats through side

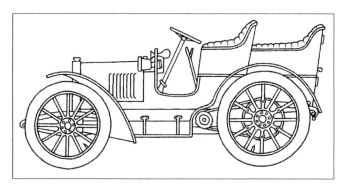

²Tonneau. This Rear-entrance Tonneau automobile from the first decade of the 20th century developed eventually—via the Phaeton/Double Phaeton and Touring Car/Tourer—into the Cabriolet.

doors. Indeed, some light short wheelbase cars are known to have been built as rear entrance Tonneaus in spite of having propeller shaft drive to the rear road wheels. The inconvenience for the rear-seat passengers to step in from or out into what were often muddy roads and the difficulty for the coachbuilder to produce a forward foldable top with provision for a central door at the rearmost part of it, meant that the eclipse of the side drive chains in favor of the propeller shaft drive combined with lengthened wheelbases were welcome improvements for both coachbuilders and passengers. These changes enabled the introduction of side rear doors and a simplified folding top without an opening in it. Some chain-drive cars had indeed provided access to the rear passengers' seats via one of the front passengers' seats, which could be swung out for access. (This worked well with right-hand drive in European countries with left-hand traffic, but could not have been very practical with the then common right hand drive cars in old world Continental Europe which, with some exceptions, employed right hand traffic.) With the subsequent propeller-

shaft rear-wheel drive no hindrance for arranging side doors for rear passenger existed. Also, the name Tonneau stuck, for after the rear-entrance production period ended, and even when the rear seats no longer had the "tonneau" form, vehicles of similar style were for some time still termed Tonneau. Later, though, the changed character of the bodywork led to the term Double Phaeton; in fact, as soon as side rear doors were provided the transition from building the Tonneau style of bodywork toward the Double Phaeton started. Such overlapping of style terminology was not unusual.

Roi des Belges; ¹*Tonneau* ←
Important period
1899–1910.
Variations
After 1904 some specimens, in spite of chain drive, were constructed without rear entrance, the side-entrance to the rear seats being made possible by either of two expedients: swinging the front passenger's seat outwards or moving the complete bench or two front seats, as the case might be, laterally on rails to give access from one side or the other to the rear seats. A few Tonneau vehicles are also known to have been built with side rear doors in spite of a chain drive front sprocket, the covering box for which served as a step to the fairly high door sill. One car company is known to have built Rear-entrance Tonneau automobiles which had neither side chains nor large rear wheels and, therefore, could probably well have been con-

structed with side doors. The Demi-tonneau version is in effect a Voiturette *(q.v.)* with rear passenger seating for strictly two passengers. Some Tonneaus could be fitted with a detachable roof or hard top. On some of the less luxurious vehicles, the rear seats could be removed *(see Tonneau démontable)* and the space utilized for cargo.

Language varieties

Tonneau denoted initially the rear section only of the car, but subsequently the complete car. Tonneau seems to have been, and still is, an internationally used term for this style of bodywork.

→ *Double Phaeton*

[3]Tonneau

In American parlance, especially between the two World Wars, Tonneau indicated the rear part (deck) of an open car, or alternatively the entire rear seating compartment.

[4]Tonneau

Tonneau-cover.

Tonneau-cover

Today "Tonneau," or "Tonneau-cover," has come to mean a flat canvas cover at belt-line height stretched over an open Touring Car's entire rear part or an open sporting two-seater car's cockpit.

Language varieties

American: Tonneau-cover.
British: Tonneau-cover.
French: Couvre-tonneau.
German: Persenning.
Italian: Tonneau-cover.

Tonneau démontable

A Tonneau car from which the rear seats could be removed to make space for cargo or luggage.

→ *[2]Tonneau*

Top

American for the roof, folding hood and upper part of the passenger compartment; head. Alternative term: Greenhouse.

→ *Greenhouse*

Torpédo

A usually sporting two- to seven-seater Touring Car embodying the Torpedo bodywork style.

Origins and history

The term Torpedo (spelled in the

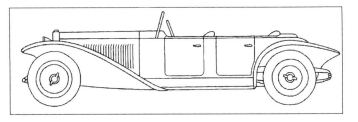

Torpédo. Both small and large Torpedo-style Touring Cars were produced mainly in the period between the two World Wars. The illustration shows one of the more expensive coachbuilt variations.

English/German way) had its origins in Germany. Those cars that sported a windshield at all before 1910 had it usually connected directly to the rear end of the engine room hood or, in the case of a rear-mounted radiator, to its rear face, and always quite far forward of the driver. Attempts to lengthen the hood or to bring bodywork panels closer to the driver had been made already at the end of the 19th century, but generally with little practical impact. On racing cars, with increasingly higher speeds, the need to deflect away dust from the

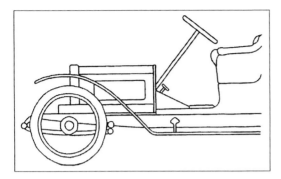

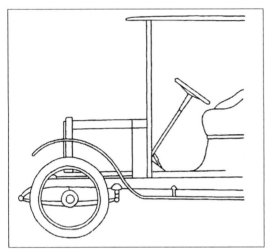

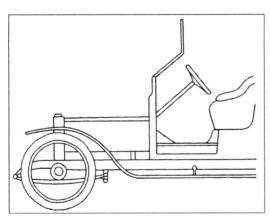

Torpedo development. *Top:* Early automobile without either cowl (scuttle) or windshield.

Middle: Torpedo development. Early automobile without cowl (scuttle) with windshield far forward of the chauffeur.

Bottom: Torpedo development. Early automobile without cowl (scuttle) with angled windshield closer to the chauffeur.

faces of the driver and mechanic became obvious during the first decade of the 20th century. Thus, some racing cars were fitted with various rudimentary cowls to extend the engine hood backwards and upwards closer to the driver; examples include the Gobron-Brillié car participating in the French Grand Prix in June 1906 and the Delages in the Coupe des Voiturettes in October 1907.

During the first "Prinz Heinrich-Fahrt" race for Touring Cars in 1908, instigated by the Prussian motor car enthusiast Prince Heinrich, these hoods, lengthened by adding cowls, or scuttles, became widely observed and were perceived at the time as torpedo-like, particularly those of the participating Horch cars. It appears that subsequently the German and French equivalents of the "Torpedo-hood" started to be used, and several alert coachbuilders began producing car bodies incorporating Torpedo cowls and moving the windshield much farther backwards. Especially with cars that still had no front doors (before approximately 1912), however, in comparison with the aforementioned racing and touring cars these initial attempts looked most ungainly. For development from no scuttle at all to the Torpedo-hood, *see accompanying illustrations.*

The Torpedo-hood term later became shortened to just Torpedo and finally that name was even used to denote the style of the complete car bodywork, especially the later versions with three or four doors and seating integrated with the

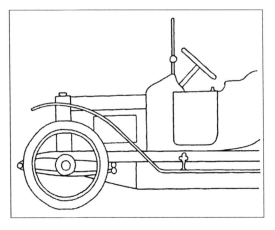

Torpedo development. Early automobile with cowl (scuttle) and windshield close to the chauffeur.

bodywork. Interestingly, the Germans themselves applied this term only sparsely to their vehicles. One example is the German car company of Beckmann & Cie in the old German town of Breslau (to-day Wroclaw in Poland) which produced in 1912 a 25/50 hp Touring Car designated "Torpedo Doppelphaeton," no doubt to emphasize the modernity of the Torpedo-style hood. Typically, but by no means initially, the body line of the French Torpédo car became more or less continuous from the top of the hood side walls rearwards along the body belt-line; a "through-line." It was in France and Italy that the term Torpedo became mostly used as a definition of this body style. The French added an acute accent and applied the name after World War I and during the next 15 years to almost any kind of open car with a modicum of sporting looks.

Double Phaeton ←

Important period
1910 to ca. 1930.

Variations
The name Torpedo was used in the United States and by some coach-

builders in England in the first years of the 1910s, but only a few embodied a smooth transition of the hood line via a cowl or scuttle to the main bodywork. The French and Italian Torpédo has two or four doors and seats normally five, or, with foldable extra seats, up to seven. Like the British Tourer it sometimes has no driver's door. Further similarities between the Anglo-American and the Continental Torpedo are the simple, soft side-screens and unsophisticated folding top. Some French and Italian cars termed Torpedo were very sporting, and some two-seater specimens were in effect Sports Cars.

Language varieties
Phaeton, Torpedo and Tourer are all known to have been used variously and indiscriminately in Europe for almost the same automobile bodywork style. In Italy the term Torpedo was used roughly in the same way as in France but spelled Torpèdo. Since the term Torpedo seems to have been used very little in the USA and Great Britain, and really only during the early 1910s, the nearest normal American equivalent would be Touring Car, and in Britain Tourer.

American: Touring Car.
British: Tourer.
German: Torpedo.
French: Torpédo.
Italian: Torpèdo.
→ *Touring Car*

Torpédo Bateau

French bodywork designation to specify the combination of a Torpédo general bodywork outline with a pointed boattail.

→ *Bateau; Torpédo*

Torpédo Grand Sport, Grand Sport

French for a 1920s Sports Tourer. Later, after dropping the Torpédo part, termed just Grand Sport. Abbreviation: GS.

→ *Sports Tourer*

Torpèdo Sport, Torpèdo Gran Sport

Italian for a 1920s Sports Tourer. Later usually termed Gran Sport.

→ *Sports Tourer*

Tourenwagen

German for Touring Car.

→ *Touring Car*

¹Tourer

British for Touring Car. An open, rather sporting type of automobile, initially without windshield and doors, usually for two people only, to sit on a bench seat. For weather protection it had a basic foldable Victoria-type top, and later doors and simple, detachable canvas side-screens secured to the body by means of pegs and sockets. An extra seat for a third passenger was sometimes provided, cloverleaf style for example (*see Cloverleaf*).

Origins and history

The two- or (sometimes) three seater Tourer evolved from the earliest and simplest form of motor propelled conveyances when "bodywork" consisted of nothing more than perches for seating and a hood to cover the engine, when the engine was not hidden mid-chassis.

²Phaeton ←

Important period
1906–1939

Variations

The Tourer underwent innumerable permutations over many years as regards bodywork detail, foldable top styles, passenger seating and arrangements for carrying luggage.

Language varieties

The American two to three seater Touring period equivalent was the Roadster *(q.v.)*. In Great Britain, the two-seater Tourer body style is often referred to simply as "2-seater." Quite often in Europe, early non-sporting two-seater cars, which were for all intents and purposes Touring Cars, were given the hyperbolic label "Sport." Also, some British two-seater Convertible cars (*see ³Cabriolet*) are known to have been erroneously referred to as Tourers.

American: Roadster.
British: Tourer, Two-seater.
French: Torpédo, Torpédo Tourisme or Voiture de Tourisme 2/3 places.
German: Phaeton, Tourenwagen 2/3 Plätze.
Italian: Vettura Turismo, Torpèdo 2/3 posti.

²Tourer

For the more common multi-passenger Tourers seating between four and seven see *²Touring Car* .

¹Touring

Touring, as a car model designation, has been and is still being used by car manufacturers all over the world for all kinds of bodywork styles. In most cases the nearest meaning of the word ("participation in a tour" or "a journey visiting interesting places along the route") has very seldom anything to do with the bodywork style in question. Before World War II Touring was mostly applied to open cars whereas more recently it has been applied to some Station Wagons and Sedans—enclosed cars whose main purpose is much more mundane than Touring.

²Touring

Touring was the well-known name of an Italian coachbuilding company (which may lead to confusion in body style contexts).

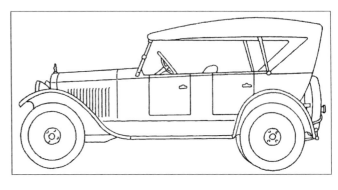

²Touring Car. An early 1920s ubiquitous American Touring Car.

³Touring

The subtype designation "T," for Turismo/Tourisme, exists mainly in combination with "G" and "i" *(see GT, Ti).*

¹Touring Car

Whereas the British Tourer and its Continental counterparts (Torpédo, Tourenwagen, Vettura Turismo etc.) did exist in two and three seater form, in the United States the term Touring Car was used exclusively for the larger bodywork version, seating between four and seven passengers. The American two or three seater Touring period equivalent was the Roadster *(q.v.).* (For European two to three seater Touring cars, *see ¹Tourer.)*

²Touring Car

An open, usually four- to five-passenger automobile having two, three or four doors, a fully extensible folding top and simple, roll-down, detachable or fold-down side-screens secured to the body by means of pegs fitting into sockets. Some larger Touring Cars had two foldable occasional seats or three permanent rows of seats providing seating capacity for seven passengers. Some—mostly European and right-hand drive Tourers—had a spare wheel on the driver's side running board instead of a door, rendering the body a three-door one. American high-class production Touring Cars and generally coachbuilt specimens are known to have been provided with a secondary windshield directly behind the front seats, Dual-cowl Phaeton-style. This was usually adjustable for height and could be folded or wound down flush. A Touring Car was obviously by definition intended for touring although its very open design did not always lend itself well to very long-distance travel. A separate rear trunk or running board mounted trunk(s) for luggage was an extra figment on some—usually coachbuilt—cars. It was not uncommon with early European vehicles to have a case for tools fitted to the front part of the floorboards, especially on the front passenger side which would usually be unoccupied by a spare wheel.

Origins and history

The multi-passenger Touring Car is generic and one of the most important open auto body styles. It evolved in America from the two-seater 18th and 19th century Buggy carriages via the Runabouts of the earliest years of the 20th century and the subsequent Roadsters to become in the late 1910s and

1920s the most common of car body styles. Likewise, the European Tourer emerged from the early Light cars, the Duc and the two-seater Phaeton style of vehicle. Two of the very early and influential bodywork styles for the capacious European Tourers were the Tonneau and Roi des Belges body styles, which were more or less superseded by the Double-Phaeton, which again was contemporary for some years with the Touring Car/Tourer on both sides of the Atlantic. Eventually, the Touring Car/Tourer name established itself as a general opposite number to the early enclosed automobile. Particularly in Continental Europe, the later Tourers showed an evident transition to the Torpedo *(q.v.)* body style. Later, requirements for improved weather protection led to the gestation of the All-weather Touring Car (from which sprang the Convertible/Cabriolet coachwork styles).

Phaeton ←
Important periods
USA: 1902–1932
Europe: 1910–1939
Variations
There were a huge number of variations as regards bodywork details, foldable top styles (some early ones giving shelter to the rear passengers only and some fully extensible ones lacking a windshield's front support), passenger seating, arrangements for carrying luggage, and other elements. In the first decade of the 20th century some American multi-passenger Touring Cars were produced without a top. These were often, mistakenly, termed Roadsters. A term variation was Phaeton, which some American manufacturers in the 1930s chose to apply to their perfectly normal looking Touring Cars. Some of

the famous British Tourers from the twenties are very sporting Sports Tourers *(q.v.)*. From the early 1930s the British Tourer often had cutaway driver's and front passenger's doors. The early Phaeton was essentially a Touring Car *(see ³Phaeton)*.

Language varieties
In the period approximately 1920–1939 in Europe the names Phaeton, Torpedo and the European equivalents of Touring Car are known to have been used variously and indiscriminately for all automobiles answering to the Touring epithet.

American: Touring Car.
British: Tourer.
French: Torpédo, Torpédo Tourisme or Voiture de Tourisme.
German: Phaeton or Tourenwagen.
Italian: Torpèdo or Vettura Turismo.
→ *All-weather*

Touring Limousine

A large, mostly chauffeur driven, Limousine for long-distance travel, with division glass and seating for three to five passengers in the passenger compartment. Early vehicles had good facilities for carrying luggage on the roof whereas later cars were provided with a large trunk. The bodywork of this type of automobile was usually coachbuilt.

Berline de Voyage ←
Important period
1915–1960
→ *²Limousine*

Touring Sedan

American for a 1930s closed, usually four-door, six side-windowed automobile having an integral "hump-back" style trunk. When the trunk became universal this term lost its importance but remained in use by some manufacturers, for, in effect, standard Sedan-bodied cars until the outbreak of World War II.

Tout-terrains

French for Off-roader.

→ *Off-roader; Voiture Tout-terrains*

Town Cabriolet

Alternative designation for the Convertible Town Car body style. *See Convertible Town Car.*

Town Car

Town Car is the American term for Coupé de Ville. The Town Car had an enclosed luxurious compartment for two or three passengers, sometimes with foldable extra seats. Generally there were two side windows only. The chauffeur's seat was in the open with a removable roof section, and there was always a division glass. Front doors were sometimes provided with windows to give driver protection in inclement weather. The bodywork of these cars was usually constructed by custom body builders. Some American manufacturers favored the name Brougham for this style of automobile but, to be correct, there are body style characteristics to differentiate a Brougham from a Town Car or Coupé de Ville *(see ²Brougham).*

Origins and history

The origins of the Town Car go back via the French Coupé de Ville body style and the Coupé to the Berline automobile which descended from the French horse-drawn Berline carriage conceived in the 17th century in the German town of Berlin.

Coupé de Ville ←

Important period

1910s up to World War II.

Variations

A larger style of Town Car, characterized by having a more spacious passenger compartment with usually two side windows on each side and a passenger capacity of five or six is called a Limousine Town Car (for illustration, see *²Coupé Limousine*). Another variation was the Convertible Town Car with completely foldable passenger compartment top. A Town Car with a folding roof section over the rear Quarter only was sometimes, probably mistakenly, termed a Cabriolet Town Car, but was in effect a Landaulet body style. (Town Sedan was a name sometimes applied by American auto manufacturers in the decades before and after World War II to open drive Town Cars as well as those having the chauffeur's compartment fully enclosed.) Subsequently, when the chauffeur was allowed a fixed roof and the comfort of complete enclosure, the body style, still with a glass division, became a Limousine.

Language varieties

American: Town Car, Brougham.

British: Brougham.

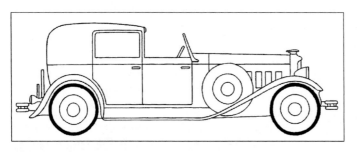

Town Car. This was the normal Town Car body style (which did not exhibit the Brougham bodywork characteristics).

French: Coupé de Ville, Coupé Chauffeur.

German: Stadt-Limousine.

Italian: Coupé di città, Coupé de Ville.

Town Sedan

Town Sedan was, somewhat unaccountably, applied as a name by some American auto makers in the decades before and after World War II to quite normal Town Car bodywork styles, both open drive and fully enclosed ones.

Town Car ←

Transformable Brougham, Transformable Limousine Brougham

Coachbuilders sometimes applied the name Transformable Brougham or Transformable Limousine Brougham to a Brougham automobile having the facility of completely enclosing the chauffeur's compartment, by wind-up side windows and canopy roof *See* ²*Brougham.*

Transformations-Kabriolett

German for All-weather Touring Car.

→ *All-weather*

Tre volumi

Short for Carrozzeria a tre volumi. Italian for Notchback.

→ *Notchback*

Tricar

A simple small open three-wheeled motor vehicle, in Britain usually referred to as Three-wheeler, having either a single front wheel or a single rear wheel. It could have either front wheel drive or rear wheel drive. Tricars have been designed and built since the advent of motoring. The first period of Tricars ended around 1910. They were succeeded by the proper Light Car which appeared after World War I *(see Light Car; Voiturette).* In the specialist world of British Kit Cars the Three-wheeler—with two at the front—is enjoying a renaissance.

Tricycle ←

Triciclo

Italian for Tricycle

→ *Tricycle*

Tricycle

An early three-wheeled very light open motor vehicle having a single front wheel and usually single cylinder air-cooled engine hung behind the rear axle. It had light cycle type wire spoke wheels and rear-wheel drive. The contemporary motorcycle was a difficult machine to handle on the bad roads at the end of the 1890s and therefore the motor Tricycle became an important and preferred vehicle well into the first decade of the 20th century. Its total lack of bodywork is not to be sneered at—

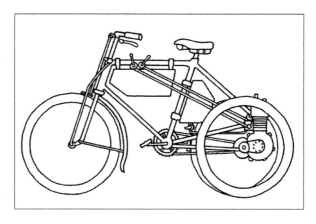

Tricycle. A popular early motor vehicle when roads were too bad for motorcycles.

quite a few race drivers of the day had their first experience in high speed driving at the handlebars of a Tricycle.

American: Tricycle.
British: Tricycle.
French: Tricycle.
German: Dreirad.
Italian: Triciclo.
→ *Tricar*

Trike

Alternative term, somewhat colloquial, for Tricycle.

American: Trike.
British: Trike.
French: Tricycle.
German: Trike.
Italian: Triciclo.

Triple Phaeton

An early open seven- to nine-passenger automobile with three rows of comfortable seats and a large but simple foldable top. Otherwise similar to a Double Phaeton, but access to the rearmost seats was arranged either through a gap between the two seats of the middle row (which could be fitted with an occasional seat) or with an extra set of rear doors. The illustration shows the former system.

Origins and history

It would be reasonable to assume that the Triple Phaeton sprang from the Double Phaeton. Although a comparatively rare style of body, Triple Phaetons were produced in France, in the United States and in Germany in the period around 1910. In Scotland the St. Vincent Cycle & Motor Works built a Triple Phaeton, called, however, Tourer.

Double Phaeton ←

Important period

1910s up to World War I.

Variations

Although not using the name Triplo Phaéton, Lancia in Italy in the same period advertised a car with three rows of seats entirely open to the sides and thus with direct access to the seats without doors. Like some other vehicles with three rows of seats this vehicle had a simple, parasol style roof on pillars instead of a folding top to cover both passengers and driver (a reversed sun roof, as it were). A very tall windshield in front supported the roof. Also Swiss coachbuilder Geissberger built a fixed roof Triple Phaeton on a Dufaux chassis having glass Quarter lights. In 1907 Pratt Chuck Works in America made only one very unusual six-wheeler with three rows of seats that had all the bodywork qualifications of a Triple Phaeton. The Mack brothers built in 1904 a very large "Touring Bus" with three rows of seats plus a rear Tonneau, probably with rear entrance, giving a passenger capacity in excess of 12. Also Napier in England

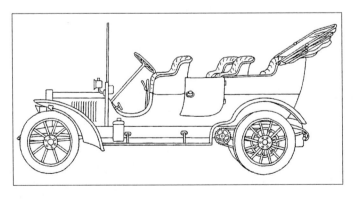

Triple Phaeton. An automobile style made in small numbers by quite a few manufacturers.

built an enormous automobile in 1912 with four rows of seats, but the term "Quadruple Phaeton" does not appear in relevant literature.

Language varieties
There appears to have been no particular term used in America and on the British isles for this style of bodywork and its varieties.

American: Touring Car.
British: Tourer.
French: Triple Phaéton.
German: Trippelphaeton.
Italian: Triplo Phaéton.

Triple Phaéton
French for Triple Phaeton.
→ *Triple Phaeton*

Triplo Phaéton
Italian for Triple Phaeton.
→ *Triple Phaeton*

Trippelphaeton
German for Triple Phaeton.
→ *Triple Phaeton*

Triumphwagen
German for Chariot for triumphal processions.
→ *Chariot*

Trois places en trèfle
French for Cloverleaf seating.
→ *Cloverleaf*

Trois volumes
Short for Carrosserie trois volumes. French for Notchback.
→ *Notchback*

T-roof, T-bar roof, T-top
A longitudinal bar on an open, often two-seater car connecting the windshield header with a so-called Targa-bar on fairly wide B-pillars, thereby increasing the longitudinal strength of the bodywork structure. This body style on a few auto makes allows the fitting of removable, rigid roof panels between the windshield and the B-pillars, making the car enclosed.

Targa, Targa-top ←
Important period
1970s and 1980s.
Language varieties
Italian: T-roof.

Turismo
Italian for Touring.
→ *Touring; Touring Car*

Turismo Internazionale
Full name for Ti/TI.
→ *Ti*

Two-box
Alternative term for Fastback, applicable in American English, British English and Italian.
→ *Fastback*

Two-plus-two (2+2)
Usually a somewhat longer wheelbased front- or rear-engined Sports Coupé *(q.v.)* with a rear seat to accommodate two passengers. Rear seat room is cramped, however, distinguishing this style from a four-seater.

Origins and history
The Two-plus-two often derives from an initially pure two-seater sporty car or Sports Car. Modern Two-plus-two cars are powerful enclosed four-seaters with full electric and electronic comforts.

Sports Coupé ←
Important period
Circa 1960s to present.
Language varieties
American : Two-plus-two (2+2).

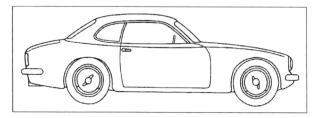

Two-plus-two. The 2+2 Sports Coupé is a nice alternative for the family driving enthusiast.

British: Two-plus-two (2+2).
French: 2+2 places.
German: 2+2 Sitze.
Italian: Due + due.

Two-seater

Two-seater was an old and easy British way of referring to a Roadster style of automobile as defined under [3]*Roadster* and [1]*Tourer* . *The Motoring Encyclopedia & Touring Gazetteer* of 1934 explains further: "This form of body is very widely used, and the seat is often wide enough to accommodate three persons. Nearly all two-seater bodies are fitted with a folding double dickey seat." (The implication is, of course, that the vehicle is open and has a folding top.)

-U-

[1]Undercarriage

Assembly of frame members, suspension, wheels and other components forming the framework that supports the body of a horse-drawn carriage or motor vehicle. Alternative term: Chassis.

➙ *Carriage; Chassis*

[2]Undercarriage

The landing gear of an airplane.

Underslung

English for a low-built automobile chassis with live road wheel axles, where the (usually half-elliptic) springs were

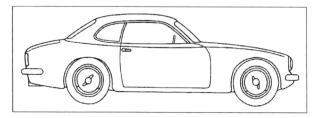

Underslung. An advanced American chassis design in its day, giving a low center of gravity. Unfortunately it was not produced in any significant numbers.

located under one or both axles. This term was also used to describe an even lower chassis where one (usually the rear) or both axles were located above the chassis frame members. The consequence of a low chassis is very often, if not always, a low body style. In the first two decades of the 20th century a few American auto manufacturers (e.g.

American and Norwalk) produced some very advanced and sporty Underslung Roadster and Touring style cars. (For comparison with a traditional chassis design, *see illustration of Voiturette*.) With the introduction of independent suspension systems and Unitary construction this term has lost its significance.

→ *Low-chassis; Surbaissé*

Unitary construction

A construction method in which the bodywork is built integrally with the traditional chassis units into one unit. This unitary principle is designed to provide the basis for engine, suspension, steering etc., giving both strength and low weight to the car. Early examples were the Lancia Lambda in the 1920s and the Citroën 7B in the early 1930s. Today, the various components are built on a Platform *(q.v.)*.

American: Unitary construction.
British: Unitary construction.
French: Carrosserie autoporteuse or Monocoque.
German: Selbsttragende Karosserie.
Italian: Monoscocca or Carrozzeria autoportante.

-V-

V

Italian subtype designation; abbreviation for Veloce, meaning "fast" and applied to sporty vehicles. Also used to call attention to many valves per cyclinder.

Van

According to Webster's dictionary Van is short for caravan and is "a usually enclosed wagon or motortruck used for transportation of goods or animals." It is also used internationally as an abbreviation for and in the contemporary meaning of Passenger Van *(q.v.)*.

Véhicule amphibie

French for Amphibian vehicle.
→ *Amphibian vehicle*

Veicolo anfibio

Italian for Amphibian vehicle.
→ *Amphibian vehicle*

Vettura a tetto rigido

Italian for Hardtop.
→ *[1]Hardtop*

Vettura da caccia

Italian for Shooting Brake.
→ *Shooting Brake*

Vettura da corsa

Italian for Racing Car.
→ *Racing Car*

Vettura di Piazza

Italian for Fiacre.
→ *Fiacre*

Vettura Trasformabile

Italian for All-weather Touring Car.
→ *All-weather*

Vetturetta

Italian for Light Car.
→ *[1]Voiturette*

¹Victoria

A light open four-wheeled horse-drawn, always coachman-driven, summer carriage with one rear bench for two passengers and one forward folding hood, called a Victoria hood. Usually no rear Spider (Rumble) seat. For the coachman in front there was a raised outside seat usually having only a low backrest if any. The wide and low entry was eminently suitable for the contemporary ladies' crinoline (Sallmann, Blomquist).

Origins and history

The origins of the Victoria carriage can be traced via Landau to the Calèche.

Landau ←

Variations

This style of carriage, usually with a Spider seat was on the Continent termed, somewhat inconsistently, Milord (or Mylord). A related but shorter wheelbase carriage with a rear Spider seat was on the Continent mostly known as Spider *(q.v.)*.

Language varieties

American: Victoria.
British: Victoria.

French: Milord.
German: Viktoria, Milord or Mylord.
Italian: Mylord, Victoria.
→ ¹Milord

²Victoria

A light, open two-seater or a larger four-seater automobile (illustrated). Very early horseless Victorias were

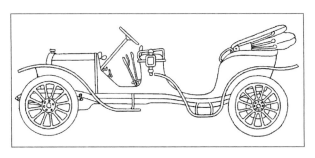

²Victoria. French Berliet made this automobile, the rear body part of which faithfully followed the bodywork design of its horse-drawn predecessor.

modelled much after their horse-drawn counterparts, complete with the Victoria type of hood, whereas later versions were usually luxurious two-door four passenger Convertibles, sometimes designated Convertible Victoria (which should not be confused with the semi-open top style—see ³Victoria below). Victoria hoods on expensive automobile chassis sometimes sported a curtain to be pulled down from the forward top portion of the hood to give protection in inclement weather.

³Victoria

A two-door Convertible car with a semi-foldable top in the 1920s and 1930s. In American parlance with a *calash* top over the rear seat only. Convertible Victoria is a fitting term for this hood position.

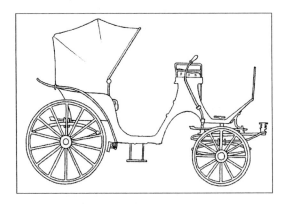

¹Victoria. A horse-drawn carriage still popular with tourists.

This style has sometimes been termed Milord.

→ *Convertible Victoria*

[4]Victoria

Although historically denoting a foldable top for open vehicles, Victoria is a designation that both auto manufacturers and custom body builders have long applied, fondly and inconsistently, to all kinds of open and enclosed bodywork. Thus, a few American coachbuilders and auto makers before World War II gave the epithet Victoria to some of their luxurious Club Sedan, Convertible and Coupe bodyworks. After the war, some American series produced high-class two-door Brougham and Convertible Coupe cars were also called Victoria. American Ford, starting in the early 1930s and continuing to the present day, attaches the name Victoria with some measure of consistency to various models, mostly enclosed two-door bodied cars but also, since the mid–1980s, to a large Sedan. Also in Italy the term Victoria has been used for some auto models.

[1]Vis-à-vis

French for a four-seater horse-drawn carriage with face-to-face seating. The front passengers were seated facing backwards and the rear passengers were facing forward.

[2]Vis-à-vis

A very early car with face-to-face seating, having a front seat for one or two passengers and a rear seat for the driver and one passenger. The driver operated the vehicle from the rear right seat and the front passenger, or passengers, sat facing backwards in front of the driver (and avoided seeing all the near-misses with pedestrians who had not yet come to terms with the horseless carriage).

Origins and history

The layout with face-to-face seating originated with various four-seater horse-drawn carriages. The Duc motor vehicle derived from the Vis-à-vis.

[1]Vis-à-vis ←

Important period

1890–1902

→ *[2]Duc*

Voiture

French for a vehicle for transporting persons or goods (originating from Latin "vectura," meaning the activity of transportation). Voiture, therefore, could infer a railroad car as well as a horse-drawn carriage and an automobile.

→ *[6]Car*

Carriage ←

Voiture Décapotable

French for an automobile with a folding or collapsible hood; i.e., Cabriolet. According to Henri-Labourdette, to be strict, Décapotable implies the ability to open an enclosed vehicle, whereas Cabriolet involves the ability to enclose an open vehicle. The tautological combination Cabriolet Décapotable is not unknown in France.

→ *Cabriolet*

Voiture Décapotable à 7–9 places

French for Convertible Stretch-limo.

→ *Convertible Stretch-limo*

Voiture Découverable

French for Sunshine Saloon.

→ *Sunshine Saloon*

Voiture de Course

French for Racing Car.
→ *Racing Car*

Voiture de Tourisme

French term corresponding to Touring Car.
→ *Touring Car*

Voiture Grand Routière

French variant term for Grande Routière.
→ *Grande Routière*

Voiture Grand Tourisme

French for Gran Turismo (GT). Alternative term: Grand Tourisme.
→ *Gran Turismo*

Voiture Hippomobile

French for Carriage.
→ *[1]Carriage*

Voiture Légère

French for Light Car, the next size larger than the Voiturette.
→ *[1]Voiturette*

Voiturelle

Name originally given by French Light Car manufacturer Decauville to their Voiturette cars.
→ *[1]Voiturette*

Voiture Tout-terrains

French for a four-wheel drive cross-country vehicle.
→ *Off-roader*

Voiture Transformable Tous Temps

French for All-weather Touring Car.
→ *All-weather*

[1]Voiturette

French term for both Cyclecars and Light Cars. The early French Cyclecar style of Voiturettes was open and quite simple, having seating in tandem or side-by-side (*see Cyclecar*). The somewhat less primitive Voiturette corresponding to the British Light Car had practically no proper bodywork, merely perched twin seats for the driver and passenger and in front a hood over the engine, or just a simple dashboard when the engine was placed underneath, mid-chassis, or at the rear. Most vehicles did sport fenders, many of which were made of wood. The name Voiturette was used to denote open as well as closed small cars.

Origins and history

The first Voiturette car was in fact a tandem-saddled three-wheeler—a Tricar, with no particular bodywork at all. It had two front wheels and one central rear wheel, which was driven. It was Léon, one of three sons of French vehicle maker Amédée Bollée, who at the age of 25 in December 1895 brought out his light Tricar, which he called "Voiturette." This proved to be a successful design and enjoyed victories in the early Paris-Dieppe and 1897 Paris-Trouville races (Jonckheere). Further race successes and record runs made the name Voiturette well known, and Léon Bollée had the courts declare that he had a proprietary interest in the name, whereupon Bollée's rival, the Société Decauville, coined for their Light car the name "Voiturelle" (Karslake).

Important period

1895–1910

Variations

The term Voiturette came to be accepted and applied after 1900 to all sorts of very light cars, one very successful design with proper bodywork and hood being the de Dion Voiturette, launched

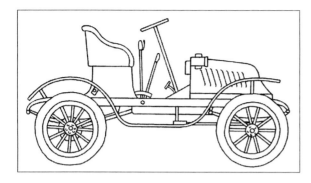

¹Voiturette. A French Voiturette from the first years of the 20th century.

in 1899. Even a Demi-tonneau *(q.v.)* is in effect a Voiturette, with rear passenger seating for only two passengers.

Language varieties
American (nearest): Buggy, Runabout.
British: Light Car, Spider.
French: Voiturette, Voiture Légère.
German: Kleinwagen.

Italian: Vetturetta, Charrette.
→ *²Buggy; Cyclecar; Light Car; ²Spider; Tricycle*

²Voiturette
The term Voiturette was also used as a racing classification formula for small race cars, formally from 1898 (though it did not start in practical terms until 1906) until 1946 (when the classification formula was changed to Formule 2).

Volume
French and Italian for the bodywork term Box.
→ *Box*

-W-

Wagen
German colloquial alternative for Car. Also German for any two- or four-wheeled Carriage of unspecified kind.
→ *⁶Car; ¹Carriage*

Waggonette
→ *Wagonette*

Wagon
→ *Station Wagon*

¹Wagonette
A very practical light four-wheeled, open, horse-drawn vehicle introduced in England in about 1845, having two usually lengthwise passenger seats facing

each other behind a crosswise driver's seat. Entry to the rear seats, which could hold four or six passengers, was through a rear door and step. The passenger seats could be folded up or removed to make space for luggage or goods. A larger, horse-drawn Wagonette was initially called a Wagonette Break, later just Break; later still it was spelled Brake.
→ *¹Tonneau 1*
³Brake ←

²Wagonette
There were some very early—late 19th century—automobile manufacturers on both sides of the Atlantic who made motor-propelled open vehicles for more

²Wagonette. The motor Wagonette had many similarities in common with the Charabanc, but it was lighter.

than six passengers, very much on the lines of the horse-drawn light Wagonette. Two passenger benches were usually arranged lengthwise behind the driver. Some of these vehicles had similarities to the heavier Charabanc and the Brake *(q.v.).*

Woodie
A Station Wagon.

Origins and history
Woodie was a name given informally by the West Coast surfing crowd in the 1960s to American Station Wagons built partly with wooden bodywork. Although Woodies were first and primarily built as a Station Wagons, after World War II the "woodie" look became fashionable and some wagon bodies were built not only of wood but also of steel to imitate the wooden look. In addition to Station Wagons, normal vehicles like Sedans and even one or two Convertible bodies were affectatiously built in the United States using veneered wood, or steel imitating wood, in the bodywork. High production costs and maintenance and care of the wooden parts on the part of the owner led finally to the demise of the genuine wooden bodies.

Depot Wagon; Station Wagon ←

Woody
Alternative spelling of Woodie.

→ *Woodie*

-Z-

Zwei-Zellenstruktur
German technical term for Fastback; alternative to Fliessheck.

→ *Fastback*

APPENDIX

The evolution of some important automobile body

Terms refer to

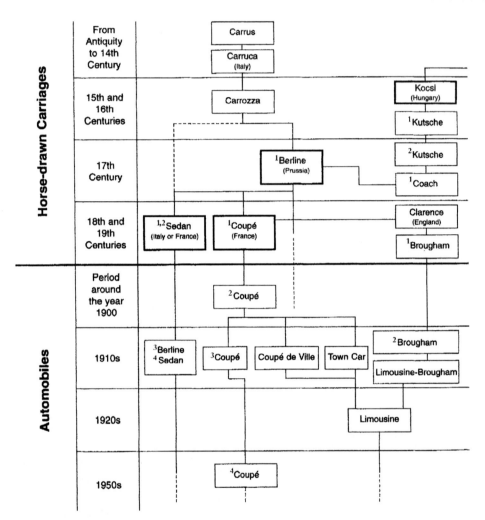

Horse-drawn Carriages	From Antiquity to 14th Century	Carrus / Carruca (Italy)
	15th and 16th Centuries	Carrozza · Kocsi (Hungary) · [1]Kutsche
	17th Century	[1]Berline (Prussia) · [2]Kutsche · [1]Coach
	18th and 19th Centuries	[1,2]Sedan (Italy or France) · [1]Coupé (France) · Clarence (England) · [1]Brougham
Automobiles	Period around the year 1900	[2]Coupé
	1910s	[3]Berline [4]Sedan · [3]Coupé · Coupé de Ville · Town Car · [2]Brougham · Limousine-Brougham
	1920s	Limousine
	1950s	[4]Coupé

styles from the age of the horse-drawn vehicle
definitions in the text.

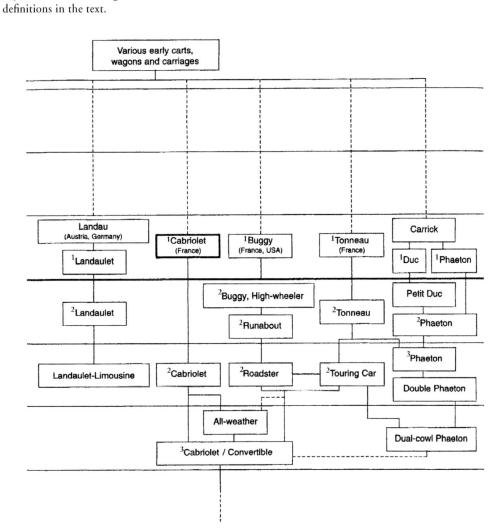

Bibliography

Books

Angelucci, E., & Bellucci, A. *The Automobile from Steam to Gasoline.* McGraw-Hill & Arnoldo Mondadori Editore (Milan), 1976.

Barker, R., & Harding, A. *Automobile Design: Great Designers and their Work.* David & Charles (Publishers) Ltd. (Newton Abbot, UK), 1970.

Belloni, L. *La Carrozza nella Storia della Locomozione.* Fratelli Bocca (Milan), 1901.

Blomquist, T., et al. *Vagnhistorisk Handbok,* Vagnhistoriska Sällskapet (Stockholm) 1998.

Boutet, J.-P. *Quelques precisions sur les termes utilisés autrefois en carosserie.* Docudep Service Technique Depanoto (Nogent-le-Rotrou, France), 1981.

Bowman, H. W., & Gottlieb, R. J. *Classic Cars and Antiques.* Trend Books (Los Angeles), 1953.

Bussien, R. *Automobiltechnisches Handbuch.* Verlag von M. Krayn (Berlin), 1928.

Butler, H. J. *Motor Bodywork.* W.R. Howell & Co. (London), 1924.

Carter, E. F. *"Edwardian" Cars.* G. T. Foulis & Co. Ltd. (London), c. 1958.

Caunter, C. F. *The History and Development of Light Cars.* Her Majesty's Stationery Office (London), 1957.

Cerri, P., & Kaltbrunner, F. *Carrozzeria italiana, cultura e progetto.* Gruppo Editoriale Electa Milano S.p.A. (Milan), 1978.

Costantino, A. *Le piccole Grandi Marche Automobilistiche Italiane.* Istituto Geografico De Agostini (Novara, Italy), 1983.

Courteault, P. *Automobiles Voisin.* E.P.A. (Saint Cloud, France), 1991.

Cronquist, A. *Ekipage.* Nordiska Museet (Stockholm), 1952.

Dalton, L. *Coachwork on Rolls-Royce 1906–1939.* Dalton Watson Ltd. (London), 1975.

Doyle, G. R. *The World's Automobiles 1880–1955.* Temple Press Ltd. (London), 1957.

Editing Committée. *Carrozzieri Italiani.* Puntografico S.p.A. (Brescia, Italy), 1997.

Fabre, M. *Hjulets kavalkade.* Danish translation from French by K.O.B. Jorgensen. Forlaget Skrifola (Copenhagen), 1966.

Fersen *see* von Fersen

Flammang, J. M., & Kowalke, R. *The Standard Catalog of American Cars 1976-1999.* Krause Publications (Iola, WI, USA), 1999.

Gartman, G. *Auto Opium—A Social History of American Automobile Design.* Routledge (New York) 1994.

Georgano, N. *The Beaulieu Encyclopædia of the Automobile.* The Stationery Office (London), 2000.

Glenning, C., Ason Holm, B., & Haajanen, L. W. *Cars of the Century.* Nordbok International (Gothenburg, Sweden), 1998.

Gottleib, R.J., & Wieand Bowman, H. *Classic Cars and Antiques.* Trend Book Co. (Los Angeles), 1953.

Gustavsson, M. *An essay in the history of design.* Konstindustriskolan (Kungälv, Sweden), 1985.

Hedinger, F. *Klassiche Wagen II.* Verlag Hallwag (Bern), 1974.

Henri-Labourdette, J. *Un Siècle de Carrosserie Française.* Edita S.A. (Lausanne, Switzerland), 1972.

Hildebrand, G. *The Golden Age of the Luxury Car: An Anthology of Articles and Photographs from "Autobody," 1927-1931.* Dover (New York), 1980.

Hill, M. *Wild Cars and Bikes.* The Hamlyn Publishing Group Ltd. (London), 1974.

Jenkinson, D. S. *Directory of Historic Racing Cars.* Aston Publications Ltd. (Bourne End, UK), 1987.

Karslake, K., & Pomeroy, L. *From Veteran to Vintage.* Temple Press Ltd. (London), 1956.

Kieselbach, R.J.F. *Stromlinienautos in Deutschland: Aerodynamik im PKW-Bau 1900 bis 1945.* Verlag W. Kolhammer GmbH (Stuttgart), 1982.

Kimes, B. R., & Clark, H. A. *The Standard Catalog of American Cars 1805-1942.* Krause Publications (Iola WI, USA), 1996.

Kowalke, R. *The Standard Catalog of American*

Cars 1946–1975. Krause Publications (Iola WI, USA), 1997.

Kozisek, P., & Kralik, J. *L&K-Skoda 1895–1995.* Motorpress + Milpo GmbH (Prague), 1995.

Locke, W.S., *Elcar and Pratt Automobiles.* McFarland & Co., Inc. (Jefferson, NC), 2000.

Mathieson, T.A.S.O. *Grand Prix Racing.* Connaisseur Automobile AB (Stockholm), 1965.

Mclellan, J. *Bodies Beautiful.* David & Charles (Holdings) Ltd. (Newton Abbot, UK), 1975.

Nerén, J. *Automobilens historia.* Motor-Byråns förlag (Stockholm), 1937.

Nesbitt, D. *50 Years of American Automobile Design 1930-1980.* Publications International Ltd (Skokie, IL, USA), 1985.

Oliver, G. A. *A History of Coachbuilding.* Cassell & Co., Ltd. (London), 1962.

Oswald, W. *Deutsche Autos 1945–1975.* Motorbuch Verlag (Stuttgart), 1981.

Parry, D. *English Horse-drawn Vehicles.* Frederick Warne (Publishers) Ltd (London), 1979.

Pfau, H. *The Custom Body Era.* A. S. Barnes and Co., Inc. (Cranbury, N.J., USA), 1970.

Pinczolits, F. *Austro Daimler.* Weilburg Verlag (Wiener Neustadt, Austria), 1986.

Robertson, C. *Coachbuilding—Past and Present.* Ed. J. Burrow & Co. Ltd. (London), 1928.

Rousseau, J. *Les Automobiles Delage.* Editions Lariviere (Paris), 1978.

_____. *Encyclopédie des Métiers "La Carrosserie." Èvolution,* Librairie du Compagnonnage (Paris), 1978.

_____, & Iatca, M. *Histoire Mondial de l'Automobile.* Librairie Hachette (Paris), 1958.

_____, & _____. *Les Plus Belles Voitures du Monde.* Libraire Hachette (Paris), 1963.

Sallmann, R. *Kutschenlexikon.* Huber Verlag (Frauenfeld, Switzerland), 1994.

Schmid, E. *Automobiles Suisses.* Èdition du Chateau de Grandson (Grandson, Switzerland), ca. 1970.

Schrader, H. *Automobil-Spezialkarosserien.* BLV Verlagsgesellschaft mbH (Munich), 1985.

Shepherd, J. *Motor-Body Building.* Cassell and Company, Ltd. (London), 1923.

Siebertz, P. *Karl Benz, ein Pionier der Motorisierung.* Reclam Verlag (Stuttgart), 1942.

Sparke, Penny. *A Century of Car Design.* Octopus Publishing Group Ltd (London), 2002.

Tarr, L. *Karren Kutsche Karosse.* Corvina Verlage (Budapest) and Henschelverlage Kunst und Gesellschaft (Berlin), 1978.

Thompson, J. *Hästvagnar.* Translation, Vagnshistoriska Sällskapet, (Stockholm), 1991.

_____. *Horse-drawn Omnibuses.* John Thompson (Fleet, UK), 1986.

_____. *Horse-drawn Trade Vehicles.* John Thompson (Fleet, UK), 1977.

Valentini, F., et al. *Lessico della carrozzeria.* Edizioni Pininfarina (Torino), 1979.

von Fersen, H.-H. *Autos in Deutschland 1885-1920.* Motorbuch Verlag (Stuttgart), 1968.

_____. *Autos in Deutschland 1920-1939.* Motorbuch Verlag (Stuttgart), 1967.

_____. *Klassiche Wagen I.* Verlag Hallwag (Bern), 1971.

Walker, N. *A–Z of British Coachbuilders 1919-1960.* Bay View Books Ltd. (Bideford, Devon, UK), 1997.

Wood, J. *Speed in Style.* Patrick Stephens Ltd. (Sparkford, UK), 1990.

Periodicals

L'Auto-journal (France).

L'Automobile (France).

Automobile Quarterly (USA).

Automobile Revue, Numéro catalogue 1961, publication annuelle (Switzerland).

Automobile Revue, Numéro catalogue 1973, publication annuelle (Switzerland).

Automobiltechnische Zeitschrift (Germany).

Automotive News (USA).

Automotive News Europe (UK).

Car and Driver (USA).

Lancia—Periodico di informazione edito e distribuito dalla Lancia & C. S.p.A. Fabbrica Automobili (Italy), 1960–1975.

Lancia Motor Club Journal (UK), No. 54 (Summer 1978).

La Manovella, (Italy) No. 1, 1981.

Mobilisti (Finland).

Motor Revue (Europa Motor) (Germany).

Motor Sport (UK), August 1953–July 1993.

Quattroroute (Italy).

Siipimutteri (Finland) No. 2/99.

Torino Motori (Italy).

The Vintage and Thoroughbred Car (UK), November 1953–April 1956.

Additionally various American, British, French, German and Italian, motoring magazines.

Articles

Automobile Revue, 1960. "Karosserieformen und ihre Bezeichnungen/Les formes des carrosseries et leurs désignations."

Chapman, D. & K. *Antique Automobile* Vol. 37, No. 6, pp. 35–40, Nov.-Dec. 1973.

de Flines, E. J. *Bugantics* (UK), Vol. 25 No. 4., Winter 1962. "French for beginners or some notes on car body or coachwork."

Garnier, P. *Bulletin de la Sociéte Industrielle de*

Mulhouse (France), No. 2/1983. "Évolution de la carrosserie automobile illustrée par les véhicules exposés au Musée National de L'Automobile."

L'Illustration, October 4, 1930. "When a Sedan is a Saloon is a Berline." Reprinted in *The Classic Car*, December 2000, pp. 8–9.

Jonckheere, N. *The Bulletin of the Vintage Sports-Car Club* (UK), No. 231, Spring 2001. "A 19th Century Lady."

Motor, May 1921. "Identifying Older Body Types." Reprinted in *Wheels*, Winter/Spring 2000, p. 2.

Encyclopædic works and Dictionaries

MOTORING

The Motoring Encyclopedia & Touring Gazetteer of the British Isles (Illustrated).
The Amalgamated Press Ltd (London), 1934.

AMERICAN-ENGLISH

Webster's Superior Dictionary, 1937.
Webster's New Collegiate Dictionary, 1979.

ENGLISH

The Collins Dictionary and Thesaurus, 1987.
The Oxford English Reference Dictionary, 1996.

FRENCH

Larousse Illustré, 1978.

GERMAN

Der Volks-Brockhaus, 1931.
Duden Deutsches Universal Wörterbuch, 1996.

ITALIAN

Italienska Ordboken, 1985.
Enciclopedia Italiana, 1937.
Lo Zingarelli, 1999, Vocabolario della Lingua Italiana.

LATIN

Latinsk-svensk ordbok, 1873.

SWEDISH

Norstedts Uppslagsbok, 1945.
Bra Böckers Lexikon, 1973.

MULTIPLE LANGUAGES

Elsevier's Automobile Dictionary in Eight Languages, 1960 (English, French, Italian, German, Spanish, Portuguese, Japanese, Russian).
Tekniikan Sanasto, 1940 (German, English, Finnish, Swedish).

Archives

Ludvigsen Library Limited, London.
Peter B. Richley, Ashford, Kent.

Museums

Le Musée de l'Automobile, Paris (France).
The Royal Stables, Stockholm (Sweden).
The Tyrwhitt-Drake Museum of Carriages, Maidstone (England).